Buy Your First Investment Property Fast

7 Steps to Successfully Acquire Rental Real Estate

Fleming Schutrumpf

Buy Your First Investment Property Fast:
7 Steps to Successfully Acquire Rental Real Estate

ISBN-13: 978-1975672638
ISBN-10: 1975672631

Published by:
10-10-10 Publishing
Markham, Ontario
CANADA

First 10-10-10 Publishing Paperback Edition September 2017
Schutrumpf, Fleming

Contents

To my son,
Alaric,

Who even when he was young and small, always
brought out the best in me,
and now that he is bigger and older,
and incredibly observant,
really keeps me on my toes.

The things I did for you
brought me more blessings
than anything I could ever have done for myself.

Foreword

If you are considering starting your own journey as a real estate investor, then *Buy Your First Investment Property Fast: 7 Steps to Successfully Acquire Rental Real Estate* is for you. This is an entertaining book that will thoroughly educate you and is an excellent guide that will set you off on the right foot in your journey towards prosperity.

Fleming Schutrumpf shares a fresh perspective on the topic of real estate in this wonderful book. Fleming's anecdotes are engaging and humorous and he makes the subject of real estate entertaining and easy to read.

Fleming is a self-taught and self-made expert in the field of real estate. You will be provided with far more than just the theoretical know-how on succeeding in the rental real estate business after you read the tales of Fleming's mistakes and the lessons he learned.

Furthermore, Fleming teaches you how to trust your intuition, set positive intentions, and believe in the good that is everywhere. I personally live a blessed life through the quality of my intentions, thoughts and actions, and through the amazing start that real estate gave me on the path to prosperity.

If you ever have the chance to see Fleming in one of his live workshops, then you should definitely seize the opportunity. You will see that Fleming is passionate and knowledgeable in the field of real estate and you will learn a great deal of perspective on how real estate can be the cornerstone of wealth.

After reading this book, you will see how Fleming combines practical applications with the laws of attraction.

Raymond Aaron
New York Times Bestselling Author

Acknowledgements

To Bob, without whom I might just own a small handful of rentals. I love your stories and your passion, and your living and breathing epitome of the Law of Attraction. Thank you for more than you can ever know you have given me.

To John Ricotta and Scott Aylor, at First Bank; Dave Adzema, at Citywide Banks; and Stacey Deuel, at Collegiate Peaks Bank. Without you guys believing in me and making purchase after purchase possible, I wouldn't be writing this book, and I wouldn't have had half the stories in here. If there is one asset every investor needs, that is a banker who believes. Thank you all, from the bottom of my heart. You represent the local banks that make our country work!

Gina, who was willing to do the right thing for me in a world where so many people are driven by commissions. Thank you for everything over so many years.

Stacy, who taught me how to interact with people better than anyone I've ever seen. Keep living your passion, yogi.

Bill Bronchick, for all the teaching and real world advice about making everything work.

Todd, for being a great friend, amazing advisor, and the best dang plumber out there.

Alan, for being an amazing connector, and for making me laugh so hard on some of the projects we worked on.

Donald Leaver, for being the best grandpa ever. Miss you!

Fleming Schutrumpf

Mom, for teaching me that work is fun, that I am handier than I would have ever imagined, and that I nosw get to do what I loved as a child: play with tools and do amazing things that are fun.

Eckart, for teaching me to work hard with my heart, to help people who need it, and to always stand up for what is right. Most of all, for supporting my dreams, and being there when I needed it the most.

Patience, for giving me the drive to get just one more, and then another, and then another.

Anna, who listened when I was speaking, and who took massive action. You inspired me to share what I know with more people. Thanks for being a go-getter.

Reda, for teaching me to ask more questions and then really listen to the answers.

Gampi, for listening to all my stories and taking action, and inspiring the first draft of this book.

Julianna, for making me hurry to finish this so you can utilize this book in your search.

Farzana, for inspiring me in so many ways. Spirituality and business belong in coexistence.

Introduction

Don't Let Fear Stop You

It is my great pleasure to share my ample collection of War Stories from about 500 tenant years of landlording experience. My goal is to both educate and entertain.

This book would be boring if the story was something like, "John went out and bought his first rental property, and he lived happily ever after collecting giant checks in his mailbox on the first of the month, every month. At the same time, his rental property increased at 15% per year, and he was last seen lounging on the beach in the Bahamas."

So, rather than telling you about lucky John, who did everything right and reaped amazing rewards, I am telling you about the real Fleming, and some examples I know of personally or through people I trust. Rather than getting you jazzed up about a fictional character and his effortless successes, I am telling you about my reality as a successful landlord. There are other books that teach the story of John. The readers of those books often lose motivation and excitement as they hit their first few roadblocks.

My job is to show you the roadblocks. More importantly, my job is to show you that you are bigger than the roadblocks. You may not love them, but you will overcome them, if you have the vision that amazing success is possible. My mentor, Bob, was my living proof that great success is possible. It would be my honor and privilege to inspire you the way I was fortunate to be inspired when I needed that inspiration the most.

I want to make sure you are not scared off by a few of the stories. To put things in perspective, I have had a very limited number of negative experiences over what I consider a very large amount of tenant years of experience. For example, I've only done maybe five, six, or seven, evictions across roughly five hundred tenant years of landlording experience, and the bulk of those evictions was due to having purchased property with existing tenants in it—bad apples who I would never have accepted if I had been the person evaluating them as applicants.

Basically, another landlord ended up with bad tenants due to bad landlording practices, which I am teaching you in this book to avoid. When I was 23, I got a discount on a 6-unit property I bought from a hairdresser in exchange for taking on the task of dealing with his tenants. In the end, I feel it was always a win for me, even when at various times it was challenging.

At one point, three of these six tenants stopped paying rent. I had to subsidize the mortgage payment with money out of my paycheck to the tune of about $1,000 a month. Yet not long later, when I sold the property, I ended up realizing a gain of $100,000. Essentially, the property had gone up $8,000 a month, even through the few months when I had been stressed about subsidizing the property out of my pocket for a small fraction of that month's gain. Who won? I did. Massively. At the time, I wasn't making $100k a year. I more than doubled my income.

In what ways did I win? I made money, yes. I made money that wasn't spectacularly easy money, so I know I earned it.

Most importantly, I learned more in that year of owning an apartment building than I learned in school from kindergarten through graduate school. And, I got paid almost every month. In the end, the real things I learned about are about perseverance, about standing up for myself, and about standing up for what is right and legal, even when *takers* try to challenge that. Then there are the transactional things I learned, such as maneuvering the legal system, maintaining and upgrading 100-year-old apartment buildings, financing, buying and selling, leasing, and screening.

The main lesson I want you to learn from this book is that if you take action, you will achieve results. If you embark on a path where there is no path back, then you will continue moving forward. If you are committed to throwing off the brass handcuffs that keep you shackled to a day job, which in the end pays just enough for you to have a comfortable means of getting rested and driving back to work the next day, this book is for you.

I bought my first rental property knowing very little. I had no concept that I would one day be self-employed, happily, as a full time investor and property manager. I didn't have the knowledge, or even the knowledge where to find the knowledge, that I am sharing here to make you successful.

Now, from where I stand looking back, I feel incredibly blessed, and incredibly driven to pay it forward, to assist other souls who want more for themselves and their families to achieve the success that is eminently achievable. I have poured my heart into this book. I feel there is so much wisdom in here from my accumulation of learning experiences over time. If you feel that you would benefit from a live seminar, please look me up on my website, at www.RentalReal EstateBook.com, and look for an upcoming training, or contact me to see about arranging one in partnership with a local Real Estate Investor's Association in your area.

Much Love
Fleming

Chapter 1

My Story About Getting into Real Estate and My Successes

"The best time to plant a tree was 30 years ago.
The second best time is now."
Chinese proverb

"The best time to buy a rental property was 30 years ago. The
second best time is now."
Adapted by Fleming from the old Chinese proverb

"He is not a full man who does not own a piece of land."
Hebrew Proverb

"I really like my life. I've arranged my life
so that I can do what I want."
Warren Buffett

"If you are interested in balancing work and pleasure, stop trying to
balance them. Instead, make your work more pleasurable."
Donald Trump

I graduated from the CU Denver School of Business in 1999 as a newly-minted MBA, and I was excited about the managerial position I thought I would soon have at the management consulting firm that I got hired on at.

To my great surprise, our team lead, whenever she was traveling out of town, appointed another woman as the acting team lead. This woman, who became my default boss whenever my real boss left town, had been the administrative assistant working the front desk for the office; her education was limited to a high school diploma and, like me, she had just recently joined our system test team, the same week I did.

Yes, she did have fairly good people skills, particularly around managing corporate politics. However, I was the newly-minted MBA, and I was willing to work harder than this individual, who bolted from the office as soon as the clock struck 5 p.m.

When this happened often enough for me to figure out there was no plan for rotating the leadership role to give the entire team a flavor of brief periods of team leadership, I resolved to take on finding my own opportunity to manage something. I figured I might as well manage something that would make me money. So, I started looking for rental property.

Having no clue how to start, I called an agent who had a property listed in the newspaper, and set up several showings for condos in the downtown Denver area that would be a good starting rental. I had rented in the same neighborhood, and knew the market, demographics, and going rates for rents. I knew it was a good rental neighborhood for students and lower-income working people wishing to live near downtown.

I proceeded to meet a mother-daughter team of real estate agents after work. At the third property we toured, a penthouse condo, they sat me down on the bed in the large bedroom with sweeping city views, and told me to sign an exclusive buyer's agreement, which obligated me to pay them $2,000 if I ended up not proceeding with a purchase within 90 days.

I felt extremely pressured by these two—pretty, but very pushy—women. I refused to sign the piece of paper and, instead, promised I would look it over and get back to them. I never did. I looked at the newspaper again and found another listing. I called the local Re/Max office that had it advertised, and then set up several showings with the agent that answered that phone, that day: Gina.

We toured several properties; one of them we could not get into. It was in a beautiful, historic building that had been converted into condos. We were able to tour several units but not that particular unit. From the stairway window, I could tell that this condo ought to have a great view of the Capitol building. However, I could not gain access to this unit; the key in the lockbox for that unit did not work. I even destroyed a couple of the store loyalty cards in my wallet, trying unsuccessfully to jimmy the lock. I had a feeling this was the best unit of the ones available, so I ended up making an offer—sight unseen. For $68,000, I acquired my first rental property, a property I only gained access to after I had already submitted earnest money to the sellers.

After purchasing that vacant condo in 1998, I immediately rented it out for $800 a month to a young woman who had just moved from Dallas to Denver.

This first rental condo is a property I still own today with great pride. I remodeled this unit extensively prior to moving into it after my divorce, and I felt blessed that despite having had this unit as a rental for 18 years, the wood floors and cabinets, and pretty much everything else, remains in great shape. I changed carpets, paint, door handles, and lighting, and added granite countertops and new appliances, such that it is likely the nicest unit in the building. I spent some happy months there. It's in an area that has great restaurants and nightlife, and proximity to museums and transit.

After my great experience with my first rental, finally having something to manage without it really seeming like any work, I was feeling successful: I proceeded to go on to buy a 6-unit apartment building, and also several other condos.

The 6-unit apartment building I bought had a lot of deferred maintenance. That was my entry point into learning how to manage contractors, do major repairs and upgrades on a shoestring budget, and deal with difficult tenants.

One important note is that if you buy a property from a very motivated seller that has tenants in it, those tenants are likely a key component to making the seller so driven to unload their property. At one point, I had three of the six units not paying rent, and I was told a non-profit legal assistance organization was giving these individuals free advice on how to stiff their landlord.

One tenant was particularly gifted at using the law in his favor. It cost me about $7,000, and 3 separate eviction filings. It also took 6 months to be able to get this tenant out, which I detail later in this book in the section on bankruptcy. I have found that individuals who I have met, interviewed, and then performed credit, criminal, and eviction screening on, have never created that kind of heartburn for me. Fortunately, it's only when I inherit or buy another landlord's mistakes that I run into situations like this. All problems can be fixed with the right amount of money; it is both important and reasonable to price any predictable factor in a rental property into your purchase price, whether it's bad tenants or a leaky roof.

Gina, who I found through a random phone call, has been a great agent for me. Gina probably handled about 40 transactions, was a key component of my team, and helped me build a substantial real estate portfolio.

4

Even after losing approximately 65% of my assets in a very difficult divorce, I ended up being left with enough to be able to be an independent real estate investor. I feel blessed to write this book to "carry it forward" and help others profit from my experience. Most importantly, I am committed to helping motivated individuals to get out of soul-crushing day jobs. All of us have the capacity to become successful business people and find a vocation that matches our purpose. I am blessed to be able to do what I consider to be my mission: providing high quality housing at fair prices to working tenants.

In 2002, my then wife was trying hard to convince me that we needed to get pregnant. I was very reluctant. It was not that long before my 401k had been decimated by the dotcom meltdown. During the glory days of rampant stock growth in 1999, I had talked to co-workers about liquidating part of my 401k to buy a Harley. Everybody talked me out of it. Not long afterwards, my 401k was smaller than what it would have been if I had bought a Harley and moved the remainder to cash, and I didn't even have a steel and chrome work of art that I could roar through the beautiful Colorado Mountains on. I had nothing to show for the transitory stock returns that came and went, even as my real estate portfolio maintained a moderate upward trend. The thing that weighed most on my mind was that, in the aftermath of the dotcom bust, my Information Technology job was looking very insecure.

Having a child to take care of instead of just being a hedonist who could jump on the Harley to roar through the mountains, or who could at whim (but only with vacation approval by the boss) take a week or two to fly to South Africa or Thailand, or China, or London, or Paris, was not something that was very intriguing to me. Yet my then wife, as she almost always did, won. After some trying, we had a beautiful baby boy, whom I love dearly. I could not have predicted the flood of hormones, the purity of love, and the depth of a deep soul yearning to take the very best care of my son. I realized so many things when my son was born: we never truly feel unconditional love until we have a helpless little child in our arms and, until we have a child, we don't know how to feel the true satisfaction of making somebody else happy. It is much better than merely trying to make ourselves happy. When we do nice things for ourselves, such as having that wonderful meal, or even buying a new car, the happiness is fleeting. When we do something nice for another, especially our children, we can smile every time we think of that moment, even if it is years later. One of the things that the birth of my son did is make me a fiercely protective dad. I resolved that I could not trust a corporation to support me in taking the care of my son that he deserves. So, I resolved to invest in real estate to create an independent stream of income that would tide my son and my family through the rough times that were likely to recur.

Our first trip out of the house with our newborn was the closing of a condo I bought as a rental. It was a great deal because it had been mislisted by an agent; he had indicated that this condo had electric baseboard heat. Electric heat is so expensive and undesirable that this type of heating system lowers property values. Fortunately, the condo was actually heated with hot water baseboard heat, fed from the common boiler, with the heat being paid through the HOA dues. Because of the inaccurate description of the condo, it sat on the market, and I was able to purchase it at a lower price than it actually justified. At the loan closing, we were joking with the closing officer that my 3 1/2 week old son would be 30 years old when that loan was paid off.

These were heady days of mortgage rates being undercut aggressively by banks, while they were also offering zero closing costs and free appraisals. As we left the closing, I saw that the credit union in the lobby advertised a rate that was a full percent lower than what I just signed upstairs at the title company. I walked in and made an application for a new loan, which closed about nine weeks later. This instant *refi* lowered my payment by about $75 a month. This equated to about $900 a year—a saving that I applied to a lot of diapers.

Later, when my son was ready for day care, my now ex-wife could not find daycare facilities that she thought were up to snuff. So, she decided to start her own child care facility. In a way, that decision of hers was the biggest gift to me ever. Through the search for a property to utilize for the daycare premises, I met my amazing mentor, Bob.

When I first met him at the property, we ended up buying from him; he was the bubbly, effervescent, energetic man who I couldn't help liking immediately. Moreover, he was firm on what he wanted. He made sure that we knew right away that he was not paying an agent commission, and that the real estate agent, who had spent more than a year helping us find a suitable property, would not be getting a commission from him if we bought his property. I felt guilty cutting Gina out of that commission on a $600,000 transaction.

Yet my sense of fairness spawned the birth my real estate empire. I resolved to buy a whole bunch of rentals to get Gina that commission back—and I did. I bought approximately 25 units from Gina in the next few years that more than offset the commissions she lost by stepping back from that deal. I believe that good things come to good people, and that includes my agent Gina. That sense of obligation to others helped me grow my portfolio tremendously.

It is beautiful when we try to help others and we can also help ourselves. That is especially true when we come from a sincere desire to help others rather than from a selfish motivation that might include others in some of the fringe benefits.

About six months after we had bought the daycare, I was purchasing a foreclosed duplex, and I hired a painter and handyman through Craigslist. He enjoyed doing the work that I trusted him to do under his own supervision while I was slaving away at my day job. He had the option of going back into regular employment, lacquering bedroom sets for a furniture factory, but told me he would have preferred to keep doing work like this for me.

I resolved to keep buying as many properties as I could with increasingly dwindling cash reserves. Soon, a Home Equity Line of Credit was frozen by Chase Banks based on concerns that the value of my personal residence, which was the collateral for this loan, had declined.

I personally get extremely jazzed up about rehabbing and fixing up properties. I spent my lunch breaks and evenings during the week, and about ten hours a day on Saturdays and Sundays, stocking supplies, checking on progress, and doing key components of the work myself. The work I did myself included everything from setting bathtubs to hanging kitchen cabinets, doors, and trim.

I get an incredible rush from seeing how a neglected property could become a beautiful property that people were lining up to be eligible to live in it. As my electrician, Alan, put it, "When you first buy some of your houses, I wouldn't let my dog go inside but, when it's done, even my brother's super-prissy girlfriend would love it." Over time, I coined my motto: "I heal hurting houses. I make unloved houses lovable again."

My mentor, Bob, taught me that when a house is vacant, it decays and degrades much faster than when it is occupied. My passion was to get houses back to where they were occupied, and where love was happening inside of them. So, I bought several more properties for my handyman, David, to maintain a steady stream of work from me. He was a reliable, trustworthy, deeply religious man, and he seemed to enjoy bringing houses back to life the same way I did.

I recall working on one stucco wall when a huge sheet of stucco fell off the brick; one of the nails, embedded in the stucco, sliced the back of my hand open, deeply, all the way to the sinew. David was kind, helping me apply Neosporin and duct tape before I slipped on a new pair of gloves and continued working. I still have that scar. It is memorable: that property is now one of my rehabs I am most proud of, and is one of the most solid returns I've achieved in my property portfolio.

Self-Help as a Tool for Learning to Believe I Can Do and Be More

Let me tell you more about Bob, who I consider to be the most inspiring mentor I've had. Bob changed my mindset entirely about real estate, yet also about so much more. In fact, without Bob, I would not be writing this book. Bob didn't just teach me about real estate. He taught me about the realm of possibility.

At our first meeting, Bob told me to purchase the audiobook, *The Secret,* by Rhonda Byrne, and *The Four Agreements* by Don Miguel Ruiz.

These are very different books, but they have a common theme. They are about believing in yourself, about integrity, and about doing your best. They are about being positive, and distancing ourselves from anything that is negative or that reminds us of what *can't* be done. These books are about having faith and trust in the Universe, and in the miracles that are around us every day.

I must have listened to the audio book, *The Secret,* a hundred times before I finally watched the video. When I first watched the video, I was quite shocked—like when you talk to someone on the telephone a lot before finally meeting them, and then you are astonished at how different they are from what you imagined. I had memorized most of the great lines in *The Secret,* along with voice tones and inflections, and had created a completely different, idealized view of how my idols looked in real life. I wonder how I would have reacted to *The Secret* by watching the movie version first.

Fortunately, I had listened to the audio of *The Secret* over and over. I listened to the point where I almost memorized it by heart, and where I suspended the disbelief I came into the self-help world with. Originally, I thought self-help was only for people who really need help. I was a moderately successfully middle manager making a healthy salary plus bonus. Surely, I didn't need that!

Yet I started realizing that some of the rich people I encountered were listening to self-help and always learning and improving. On the other hand, people who were doing just average or, worse, were "too good for that stuff" and "didn't need it." I decided to ignore what people thought about my ever growing library of inspirational and self-help titles. Having taken the messages to heart, I was starting to see, both In my private and investing life, that these messages were completely transforming my life for the better.

Does the Law of Attraction Work?

One of the memorable aspects of *The Secret,* and how our beliefs shape our reality, is a chat with a bookkeeper who worked for me. She was telling me that the law of attraction doesn't work. The law of attraction is the belief that when we allow or focus on positive or negative thoughts, we attract the results into our life that match the positive or negative quality of our thoughts. If you have ever met really lucky, happy, positive people, you might have observed that they predominantly engage in happy, positive thoughts, and vice versa for negative people.

My bookkeeper was telling me, with real certainty in her voice, that it is not possible to create wealth out of intention. She continued, telling me that thinking good thoughts does not create good results. Given how strongly she felt about this, I didn't know how to dispel her beliefs without creating an argument, which would be pointless and counterproductive.

Yet this discussion was happening as I was asking my bookkeeper to enter two new properties I had purchased recently into QuickBooks. Most importantly, these were properties that were miracles to me. These were properties that I was able to somehow buy through positive intentions, affirmations, and prayers, creating real results for me, including a down payment I didn't have and bank loans I could have easily been denied for. I got a down payment gift of $15,000 from my grandpa; it was a genuine blessing that I could never have asked for. I cannot help but strongly believe in the magic of possibilities in this amazing world we live in.

My bookkeeper's belief is true for her, while my belief is true for me. Most importantly, I like what my beliefs do for me, and do not see any value in emulating her beliefs. I'd been poor long enough; thinking thoughts that perpetuate that state is not something I wish to go back to. At the same time, I can relate to her. I used to be like her, and only when I started thinking differently was I able to transcend those old limitations.

I am forever grateful to Bob for opening me up to this world of inspirational self-help literature. If you haven't already explored the books listed above, I highly recommend those and similar resources to you.

If you can learn to suspend your disbelief and read my story, and those of other people who have come from very little to prosperity, you will know that you, too, can achieve that. Intend it and take targeted action, and you shall have it.

It sounds so easy, and it can be. Yet it's a lot like going to the gym. Some people resolve to go to the gym and actually go and get into great shape. Others resolve to the gym, but don't make it, or manage for the first four days until they get really sore, and then they never go back. The key to success in achieving your dreams is similar to getting in great shape. It takes commitment and discipline, both of which are born from the belief that you can create a positive impact in your life.

While we're on the thread of gyms, I have never had a gym membership, yet I am in excellent shape. I love remodeling properties and use that as my workout. I gladly do tasks like unloading drywall, carrying sheets alternatingly with either hand. Once I went to a naturopath who shook my hand and asked if I work out a lot. I asked why, and she commented on the slight calluses on my hands. I had to laugh, and said, "No, I actually love doing real work in the remodeling arena."

I wrote this book because I am so incredibly blessed; in this book, I hope to share my knowledge. There are so many of you who work in jobs that you aren't happy with, and so many of you who have children that deserve more. I want you to be able to step up, to seize all the possibilities available, and to create the very best life that is possible for you.

Doing Business the Enlightened Way

"Being good is good business."
Dame Anita Roddick

*"Making money is art, and working is art,
and good business is the best art."*
Andy Warhol

Here's a little more about Bob. I met him when I bought the daycare property from him. Somehow, through MBA School, I was taught that doing business was more of a zero-sum game. Instead of win-win, a zero-sum game means that for one party to win, the other party has to lose. To engage in a transaction, we would be adversaries, seated on opposite sides of the table with opposing interests. My interest would be to get the property as cheaply as possible, while Bob's interest was to get as much money as possible in the sale.

Fortunately, for both that transaction and my life since then, Bob has a completely different worldview. Bob aimed to get a fair price for the property, and he got a decent return for himself on the sale. At the same time, he also gave me a fair price on the property, but that's not all. He introduced me to a mortgage lender who made the purchase possible.

Also, we were dealing with a HOA president who was unhappy with the idea of daycare returning to that property because of the traffic impact, as well as the sound of screaming and playing children. To discourage me, one of the multiple and more unreasonable demands the HOA president made was that we stucco over the perfectly fine brick facade of the building. I mentioned this new demand to Bob at one of our meetings where he was coaching me on some of the Law of Attraction and success literature he was introducing me to.

Bob is an incredible person; he is energetic and funny, yet underneath it all he is decisive and a wonderful giver. He cocked his head as he made a rough guess at the square footage of the street-facing brick that we were being asked to stucco, and then estimated the cost per square foot. Bob then asked, "Fleming, would you allow me to credit you the amount of money to stucco this?"

This was a big gift Bob gave me. It was far more than a gift of money. It was a gift of knowing that a good businessman does business in such a way that I would be eager and honored, even lining up, to do business with Bob again.

Moreover, the next times I did business with Bob, I knew how we operated and how we treated each other, so we outdid each other in kindness to each other, and it made the transactions fun, beautiful, and an affirmation of our friendship.

This has had a lasting effect on my view of how business should really be done. The business professors at MBA graduate school, who don't do much business but stand in front of class and teach it, should have the privilege of interacting with individuals like Bob. The more I learn about truly wealthy individuals, I realize that at the upper echelons of reputable individuals, a lot of business is done based on trust, mutual friendship, and the fact that all parties to the transaction can benefit. I now employ this model with my tenants, my contractors, and the other parties that I deal with; it really works to our mutual benefit. I even find that key people in the City and County of Denver operate on the same basis, and it is so gratifying to me to find that, in government, we have enlightened people who operate in a way that is a win-win for the community and the arm of government that they represent.

How I Learned to be Handy from an Early Age

My passion for making things started early. I remember when I was growing up, accompanying my mom to the department store. While my mom was shopping for clothes, I would head straight to the toy aisle. I would find a car or truck and beg my mom to buy it. Due to our financial state while growing up, most of the time, she said, "No."

Disappointed, I would go home, where I would dismantle my old toys by taking off the wheels. I would then take various scraps of wood and my dad's tools. I would cut, file, and sand the wood pieces into shapes that resembled a truck or racecar, or whatever, and then nail on the wheels I had stripped off my old toys.

I still have scars on my hands from using a hand saw (incorrectly) when I was 4 or 5 years old. Yet this taught me a lot. Being forced to make my own toys forced me to learn to be handy.

My belief is that being good with tools is not an inborn trait. It is merely the product of lots of practice. Like the rule of 10,000 hours, spending enough time doing something will make you pretty good at it. However, most things in the remodeling realm don't require 10,000 hours to do an adequate job.

Therefore, not having plastic toys to choose from taught me how to make things that create value for me out of scraps. At the time, I had zero appreciation for this. I would have much rather had the pre-made, colored plastic toys that the rich kids had. Now, I realize that not getting toys bought for me was a key part of my foundation, leading to my current success. I was forced to learn how to improvise and look for opportunities, and to use my own sweat and, occasionally, a little bit of blood, to get what I wanted.

Chapter 2

Real Estate is the Best Investment

"Buying real estate is not only the best way, the quickest way, the safest way, but the only way to become wealthy."
Marshall Field, business man and philanthropist

"Landlords grow rich in their sleep without working, risking, or economising."
John Stuart Mill, English philosopher and economist

"Real estate cannot be lost or stolen, nor can it be carried away. Purchased with common sense, paid for in full, and managed with reasonable care, it is about the safest investment in the world."
Franklin D. Roosevelt

"If you don't own a home, buy one. If you own a home, buy another one. If you own two homes, buy a third. And, lend your relatives the money to buy a home."
John Paulson, investor and multi-billionaire

"In the real estate business, you learn more about people, and you learn more about community issues, you learn more about life, you learn more about the impact of government, probably than any other profession that I know of."
Johnny Isakson, U.S. senator

"Buy land; they're not making it anymore."
Mark Twain, writer and humorist

*"Some people look for a beautiful place.
Others make a place beautiful."*
Hazrat Inayat Khan, spiritualist

Trusting the Finance Professors:
The Cost of Not Investing in Real Estate

There's a family story that really underscores the value of real estate to me. A distant aunt and uncle lived in Stuttgart, Germany, during the 1930s, just before rampant inflation virtually destroyed the German economy. They lived with their family of four children in a beautiful, big house with an amazing garden, where they grew everything from a variety of vegetables to apples, plums, and berries.

This uncle was a professor of Finance at the University of Stuttgart. One day, out of the blue, being a healthy looking man in his early 50s, he collapsed and died from a heart attack. My aunt was not prepared for this, having been a housewife and not having been involved in the financial aspects of her household at all. After all, her husband was a professor of Finance; why should she have handled these matters?

So, she went to her dead husband's colleagues—the leading finance professors at that prestigious university. Their advice was firm: sell the house; park the money in a good savings account with a solid bank, and live off it. The new widow followed these financial experts advice. She sold the house and moved with the four, now fatherless, children into a rental which she paid for from the savings account.

Not long thereafter, rampant inflation started. You can see this inflation on the stamps dating back to this time. A stamp that previously had a currency unit of one Reichsmark was modified to have a currency unit of a hundred, which was later stamped over with 10,000, and possibly higher.

Soon, the small fortune she had gotten from the sale of the house was barely enough to buy a loaf of bread. She was left with nothing, and had to move in with other family in a distant village, where even during the hard times during the Second World War, the farmers still had a bit of food that was not as readily available to the inhabitants of cities like Stuttgart, where hunger and starvation were common.

What are some lessons from this? For me, the first lesson is be cautious about trusting the *experts*. There are lots of academic experts with great degrees and a wealth of knowledge. Yet I often see that there is a negative correlation between having substantial amounts of education, like a PhD, and actually having wealth. I can say that, because my own father is a professor. He has always been extremely hardworking, to the point of possibly being classified as a workaholic, yet had he chosen a different field, his ample efforts might have been much more rewarded.

One thing I learned from my father, that has stood me well, is that it is vital to take great pleasure in work and the achievement of results. He does it, and I do it as well.

Another lesson to me is that having too much faith in the value of currency is a risky strategy. For four years of my life, I grew up in South Africa. In 1983, when my parents and I moved there, the strong exchange rate at the time meant that it took a lot of foreign currency to buy things in South Africa.

Just four years later, after sanctions had been levied by the US government against South Africa for their continued practice of Apartheid, the South African currency had lost roughly half its prior value. The sale of assets in South Africa now netted just half of what had been paid four years earlier, seriously cramping the amount of money available to purchase a house as my family moved to Boulder, Colorado.

The scenario of unforeseen inflation and currency devaluation is not unique to German currency or the South African Rand, and not just to my own family. For example, between 1933 and 1995, according to the Foundation for Economic Education, "the U.S. dollar has lost 92 percent of its domestic purchasing power." *https://fee.org/articles/central-banks-gold-and-the-decline-of-the-dollar/*

Another aspect is that real estate cannot be easily stolen. I know many people who believe that precious metals, such as gold and silver, are a great hedge against the possibility of the devaluation of our currency. Then again, there are tons of excellent movies, from old westerns to movies like *The Italian Job,* detailing spectacular heists of gold and other precious metals.

On the local front, well outside of Hollywood, a contractor who had done a number of granite installs for me complained one day that in the same week somebody had stolen a trailer, and his house had been burglarized, with a quantity of gold being stolen; it was a presumed inside job since they knew exactly where the gold had been hidden. Real estate is not nearly as portable. Nobody can just break in and walk away with your real estate. Furthermore, there are safeguards ranging from title insurance to prenups that can protect you from losing your real estate.

The most important lesson to me is that real estate is an enduring asset. Real estate provides value regardless of the monetary value that might be assigned to it at any point in time. If my distant aunt had kept her house, she would not have had to resort to begging for shelter from relatives, probably living in very cramped conditions with her four children in a spare room. She would have been able to keep her house and garden, and the harvest that would have fed her family. Plus, she possibly could have taken in other displaced people in exchange for a rent payment that adjusted with the craziness of the inflation that was taking place at the time. Instead, my distant aunt had sold her house and was left with a pile of worthless paper.

Lastly, I wonder what that house would be worth today if it had remained in the family. The fact is that real estate becomes an even more valuable asset as our population continues to increase. In the 1930s, the world population was only 2 billion; now it is getting closer to 8 billion. The value of land and housing, especially close to urban centers, will inevitably increase as demand increases, while supply remains constant.

This is why I have dedicated myself to growing a portfolio of real estate. I have been blessed by this portfolio, and am honored to be in a place in my life where I am in a position to share the knowledge that created this blessing with you, dear reader.

Historical Real Estate Appreciation

A mentor of mine, Bill Bronchick, said a good rule of thumb for projecting future returns of real estate is to assume that real estate will double approximately every 10 years. Certainly, there are market cycles, and real estate won't always go up like clockwork but, viewed over an extended amount of time, this statistic serves as a good, rough postulate.

A beautiful aspect of this phenomenon is that if you make a mistake and buy a property for a little bit too much money, the rising market, over time, will eliminate any impact to that mistake.

I helped my little brother buy a house. I joke that he's my little brother: he is younger than me but, at 6'6", he is bigger than me. In November of 2008, he purchased a row house for a mere $34,000, adjoining one of mine, when I was tapped out for funds and couldn't afford to purchase that one. Only six years later, he sold the property for

$125,000. He was pleased as punch, and really couldn't believe that the market would continue to go up at such a steep rate. Now, three years later, the property has doubled again—it is now worth $250,000.

Keep vs. Sell: a Long-Term Perspective

My request to all my readers is to please think long-term. If my brother had held on longer to this cash flowing property, or if he would have done a refinance to pull out equity rather than selling it, he would have reaped further gains, rather than locking in a smaller windfall. Quite likely, in another say twenty or thirty years, that property could be worth a million dollars.

The problem with selling and cashing out your profits is that money, for many people, is like having sand in our hand. The sand runs out between our fingers. When we think back to big chunks of money we got two, three, or four years ago, we cannot really recall what we did with it all. Often, the money gets whittled away a little bit at a time: there's a car repair bill, then an expensive date at a nice restaurant, a new laptop (which is, by now, ready for the next upgrade), or a big screen TV (which is now starting to show signs of age, and has gotten a lot thicker than the new ones at the store). Money will come, but, without careful handling, money will go quite easily.

Yet houses, if you keep them, will stick around and grow in value. I can't think of any other investment that goes up that much. Certainly, it's not cars or vacations, or electronics, or that custom tailored suit. Please, seriously consider holding onto your real estate—nothing else appreciates as amazingly. I would rather continue living like a student or a middle-class working person on a budget than to splurge now on depreciating assets, while giving up real wealth later. Moreover, getting a check every month is far better than simply getting a big check once.

Copying Strategic Long-term Thinking from the Masters

*"Someone's sitting in the shade today
because someone planted a tree a long time ago."*
Warren Buffett

I love the Japanese business philosophy where strategic thinkers plan in 5, 10, or even 50-year time horizons—and dominate the market in the long run. Think of the history of Toyota, which was such a tiny company that in the years from 1936 to 1943, Toyota made only 1757 cars, mostly copied or even cloned from US designs. Look at Toyota now. A few years ago, Toyota became the world's number 1 automaker. Where can we go through emulating successful principles from others to absolutely dominating the market? How can we apply this in real estate?

Where can we think long-term, ignoring that we are starting small, and focus on being so good that we dominate over time?

Real Estate When I Am 80 Years Old

Furthermore, in terms of my long-term thinking about when I'm 80, I love the idea that I'll be able to get in my car, drive to a property, clip a couple of hedges for 20 minutes, maybe pick up a couple pieces of trash, do a couple things that get me a little movement, have a positive interaction with some customers, collect a rent check, do a review of one of my real estate assets, and then drive back, feeling satisfied that I put in a decent day of work for an 80-year-old.

I know, by that time, real estate appreciation will more than take care of me, and my real estate will have doubled four times in the next, roughly, 45 years. It is a good feeling, both to have just enough *work* to really enjoy my free time, and that I will not have trouble paying for a full tank at the gas station (I always feel sorry for the person in front of me when the gas pump shows that all they were able to afford to fill their car was $4 in gasoline.). I love the fact that, for me, this is not work; it's an activity that instills pride and satisfaction, and that rewards me in a multitude of ways: some, but not all of them, being financial.

How Many Properties Would Pay Your Monthly Bills?

The effect of wealth growth, over time, is startling. When mortgages eventually get paid off and you have free and clear equity in your home, as well as rent payments where the bulk now goes to you instead of the lender, you are in a great place.

Having only a few properties can take good care of you in your old age once they are free and clear of loan obligations. One mentor I talked to, who owns dozens and dozens of properties, talked about simplifying and reducing his holdings down to just 13 properties. These would be single-family houses in an upscale, college town, where each house should rent for roughly $2,000–$3,000. For a limited set of assets, that is an extremely healthy, monthly income.

There are many dire predictions about the wealth, or the lack thereof, of most Americans as they enter retirement. At the same time, The United States of America is the country that is one of the most favorable towards home ownership and towards allowing you to build a portfolio of rental properties with amazing government-subsidized loan programs. There are many Western European countries where ownership of real estate is concentrated in the upper-class, and the vast majority of the population are renters. For example, in Germany, where I was born, homeownership is around 40%, while in the US, it is around 65%. That's a huge difference. If you line up 10 people in both countries, in Germany, only 4 will own real estate. In the US, it is almost 7.

That we are fortunate enough to be living in America, and able to join what in most countries is the elite land-owning class, is such a blessing for us all. If that blessing exists, why not seize it? Become a landlord. Become wealthy. All the opportunity is here.

This book was written to teach you how!

Forced Savings through Principal Payback

The principal repayment, as part of your loan, doesn't seem like much in the first year of owning your first rental property. On one of my amortization statements, the first month's principal, on a 30 year loan, was just $57. However, over time, it starts adding up, since every payment has the interest amount go down slightly, while the principal amount goes up by that same amount.

As the amount in your mortgage payment that gets applied to principal grows, the equity in your property is growing. Initially, you start off with the bank owning a large chunk of your property, and you owning the remaining chunk that matches your down payment, which is often smaller than the bank's chunk.

Over time, property values will increase and, as you pay back the mortgage, the portion of the property the bank owns shrinks, while your portion grows. I term this *forced savings*. It's clearly not optional to make this savings contribution. Mortgage payments are due monthly. Furthermore, this is not a savings account you can easily tap into when your car transmission goes belly-up.

Yet once the amount has grown meaningfully, you could get a second loan on the property, or refinance the first loan to take that money back out. It is worth knowing that if you ever decide to refinance when your kids go to college, or whatever the occasion, the loan proceeds are tax free to you. Not just that, but there is a tax benefit to making the interest portion of your mortgage payments to boot.

Eventually You Own It Free and Clear

Eventually, you own the property free and clear. Of course, early on, banks are a huge blessing and, without them, we wouldn't be able to buy the properties we are able to own. Banks are an amazing partner. For three, four, five, or six percent, but hopefully not too much more, they will lend you a big chunk of the money you need to buy property. Recently, we've had such a bull market that property has gone up 50% in just a few short years. In the meantime, the bank has only been collecting 6%, or whatever the interest rate is. They are a much better business partner from a financial perspective than taking on an equity partner who gets 50% of your gains.

A big part to look forward to around owning property with an amortizing loan, is that eventually the loan will be paid off (This excludes interest-only loans, which I wouldn't recommend.). The loan payoff may take 30 or 20, or 15 years, depending on your loan and the size of optional extra payments you make. I purchased my first rental property in 1998. Based on having paid more than the mandatory minimum payment some of the times, when I had the means to do so, I am now set to pay off the 30-year loan, 11 years early.

Mortgage Interest Costs Explained

I realized, after reading about how loans work, that for every dollar that is outstanding in principal, I will pay the same 6% interest in year one, two, three, ... 27, 28,29, and year 30. At 6%, I would be paying $1.80 in interest over 30 years on that one dollar. So, if I can pay that dollar I was going to pay off in the final 30th year, this year, I save a lot of years in interest payments. Those savings are highest the earlier I make the prepayment. Therefore, prepaying some amount of additional principal is a great way of accelerating your mortgage pay-down.

Strategies for Accelerating Your Loan Repayment

One formula I heard was to simply pay double the amount of principal that is coming out of your normal payment. That roughly shortens the term of a 30-year loan to about 20 years, or somewhat less.

Another way to save about 7 years off a 30-year loan is to just simply make a 13th mortgage payment every year. An easy way to achieve this is by taking bi-weekly withdrawals from your account; so, even though it feels like two withdrawals a month, there are actually 52 weeks in a year and, therefore, the 26 withdrawals are equivalent to 13 months. This gives you that extra mortgage payment each year.

There are third-party providers that offer programs like this with names such as *bi-saver*. However, you can do this yourself without incurring the costs of having a third-party administrator (be aware of hidden items, like the administrator collecting your payments all year and only disbursing the lump sum at the end of December). If you really have great cash flows, consider just doubling your entire PITI (Principal, Interest, Taxes and Insurance) payment, applying the entire extra payment to principal.

One way to track how your prepayments are affecting the mortgage pay-down, is to take the amortization schedule that is handed to you at loan closing, and trace down how many months you skip when you pay an extra amount of principal. As stated earlier, especially early on in the loan, the positive impact can be significant.

A Big Savings Account vs. Prepaying Your Loan

I highly recommend first having a healthy savings account and contingency fund before you start aggressively pre-paying the loan. It is important to remember that if you ever run into a rough patch, the bank will not refund your prepayments or let you skip future payments based on past extra payments.

If you cannot make your loan payments that are due now, the bank is still in a position to foreclose. It's much better to be able to make three, six, or even twelve months of payments out of your savings than to have prepaid the same amount of money to principal, and have no money left to make continued monthly payments if there were to be an emergency.

There is an old adage about lawyers and the words "it depends." While some lawyers, especially those with a product to sell, might tell you something like "principal repayment is always a great idea," a good lawyer will almost always tell you, "it depends." Only upon understanding your full situation and the specifics you are dealing with, can one give a proper answer. It's a great idea to have cash reserves, and it's a great idea to prepay principal, but there's a balancing act between the two. You should be suspicious of formulaic advice that doesn't take your specific situation into account.

That is why, in this book, I aim to give you the considerations to consider, without trying to push you into a hard and fast course of action.

Chapter 3

The Importance of Taking Action

"Action is the foundational key to all success."
Pablo Picasso

"You don't have to be great to start,
but you have to start to be great."
Zig Ziglar

"A real decision is measured by the fact that you've taken a new
action. If there's no action, you haven't truly decided."
Tony Robbins

"Successful people maintain a positive focus in life no matter what is
going on around them. They stay focused on their past successes
rather than their past failures, and on the next action steps they
need to take to get them closer to the fulfillment of their goals
rather than all the other distractions that life presents to them."
Jack Canfield

Please, remember: the most important thing in life is to actually *take action*. It's better to take action and make mistakes and adjust, than it is to plan for perfection, and seeing that such plans are difficult to make, not executing.

One of the amazing things about real estate is that it is truly indexed for inflation. The one that gets me even more excited is that, eventually, unless you refinance your loans to take out more cash to buy other properties, or whatever you might do with the money, your loan will be paid off, eliminating that loan payment. That can have a big impact on your income. You might have a property renting for $1,300 a month. Let's assume $1,000 monthly is going to PITI, or principal, taxes, and insurance. Once the loan is fully repaid, principal and interest fall away, and your monthly recurring expenses might drop from $1,000 a month to something like $300 a month. That is a big pay raise!

I love being a long-term investor. I highly recommend that you think long-term, and look forward to the *glory days* when you will be getting a significant raise because of being a long-term thinker who makes long-term investments. Paying off a mortgage, over time, is the mark of a long-term investor. Celebrate that when you get there. In 1998, when I bought my first rental condo, I had no concept of how happy I would be getting close to paying a loan off. It is such a great feeling.

Rents Indexed To Inflation

Apartment List analyzed Census data from 1960–2014. "We find that inflation-adjusted rents have risen by 64%, but real household incomes only increased by 18%. The situation was particularly challenging from 2000–2010: household incomes actually fell by 7%, while rents rose by 12%."
(https://www.apartmentlist.com/rentonomics/rent-growth-since-1960/ accessed on July 21, 2017)

There's more: "Landlords keep cranking up rents, with annual increases far outpacing price growth elsewhere in the economy, according to data released Thursday. Rents in May were up 3.5% from a year earlier, while a gauge for overall consumer prices showed no growth, the U.S. Labor Department reported."
(http://www.marketwatch.com/story/rent-inflation-shows-no-signs-of-letting-up-2015-06-18, accessed July 18, 2017)

Clearly, this is evidence that you should be a landlord, not a renter.

Do Rents Drop During a Recession?

Tellingly, even when net household income dipped during the recession in the 2008–2010 period cited in the study, rents continued increasing disproportionately.

People often asked me about this. They remember how challenging the recession was and can't comprehend that rents would rise even as real estate values dropped. One part to this was the subprime foreclosure crisis. The sheriff would evict foreclosed homeowners, who would then need new housing to move to. The more houses were foreclosed on, boarded up, or otherwise unavailable as part of the housing pool, the more a shortage of housing was created, which increased demand for available housing, creating price growth in rents.

Cash Flows vs. the Value of Your Property

This is good news for landlords. If you are in this business for the long-term, your security is created through cash flows, not the value of your investment property. As long as monthly rents keep coming in, being able to sell the property for $30,000 or $300,000 is relatively immaterial, especially in the case of unique market conditions like the 2008 subprime mortgage crisis that created a distorted market, which has since completely recovered.

The trends in the widening gap between slower income growth and faster rent growth is significant. It proves the value of having rental real estate as a component of your streams of income.

I saw this in my own life. I worked in Information Technology, starting as a requirements analyst and, later, as project and program manager. Even as my experience, seniority, and reach grew, and I managed larger teams, my income remained steady and, later, even declined due to globalization and competitive pressures in the industry, as well as management challenges in the organization where I worked. Rent prices kept climbing during the decline in my take-home pay, strengthening my resolve to focus on my rental portfolio rather than my corporate career as the best way to have the kind of lifestyle I desire.

Untapped Wealth You Already Have: IRAs and 1031 Exchanges

There are a number of strategies of using money you already have in order to invest in real estate. The bulk of these are beyond the scope of this book. Yet there's a couple I feel I should mention briefly. One is the notion of using retirement funds to invest in real estate. If you have an IRA, you could look into rolling that over into a self-directed IRA or a Solo 401k. Research attorneys in your area who could help you with that, or network at a local REIA (Real Estate Investor's Association) and ask for names of attorneys who are well-versed in these items. You could also check my website, at www.RentalRealEstateBook.com, for a listing of attorneys I work with. For a self-directed IRA, there are some key rules to consider:

- Your self-directed IRA *cannot purchase property owned by you or most family members;* these are considered *disqualified persons.*
- You *cannot have "Indirect Benefits" from property owned by your self-directed IRA.* This means that you cannot personally use the property as a vacation home or occasional crash pad.
- All expenses related to rental property you own in your self-directed IRA (such as maintenance, improvements, property taxes, HOA fees, etc.) must be paid from the IRA.
- The income from your IRA property must remain in the IRA. The rents must be paid into the IRA bank account where they grow tax deferred, or can be used to defray expenses related to the property in your self-directed IRA.

The other strategy is called the 1031 exchange, or just a *1031*. This is a beautiful option where you are allowed to roll your entire gain from the sale of one property, tax free, into the purchase of a new property, as long as you meet certain conditions. If you purchase your first investment property, and are looking to trade up and buy something bigger, this is a common strategy. The key conditions are:

- you must have owned the property you are selling for more than a year.
- you must identify the replacement property within 45 days and close on the replacement property within 180 days.

- the proceeds from the sale of your property may not be issued to you; instead, they must be held by a qualified 1031 exchange intermediary.

There are also reverse 1031 exchanges. In this case, you purchase another property first and then sell an existing property afterward. For more information, contact a qualified 1031 exchange intermediary. Your local title company may recommend a firm or may even have a division in house that does such. Or, check my website, www.RentalRealEstateBook.com, for a listing of 1031 exchange intermediaries I work with.

Wall Street vs. Real Estate

> *"I made a tremendous amount of money on real estate.*
> *I'll take real estate rather than go to Wall Street*
> *and get 2.8 percent. Forget about it."*
> Ivana Trump

Many mutual funds charge exorbitant fees. I can remember the day I got my 401k statement and saw that the mutual fund I had placed the bulk of my money in, because of volatility in the stock market that made me nauseous, earned a return that was negative about a third of a percent.

When researching that same mutual fund outside of the returns shown inside my 401k portal, I saw that that mutual fund actually had returned a positive 2.2%. So, not only was the mutual fund collecting fees (which is to be expected), but the 401K money managers were skimming off an additional non-trivial portion, thereby taking a barely acceptable positive return and actually making it negative.

In real estate, I have done much better. I bought a property in 2010, for $69,000 that, in 2017, was valued by the assessor at just short of $300,000. Yes, timing means a lot, but the value of the asset is just a small portion of the equation. That particular property is a three-unit and, between the three apartments, monthly gross rent is roughly $2500. At thirty thousand a year in gross cash flows, I would still be ahead, even if the value of the asset was $0. But the real value has been growing, and continues to do so.

Book Value vs. Monthly Cash Flows

As a long-term investment, I don't really care all that much what the asset is worth. Yes, the value is nice. If I needed money, I could take a loan and pull up more cash but, really, what matters is monthly cash flow.

If you are able to buy properties that cash flow monthly, that is where you want to be. What's the minimum you should go for? There's no easy answer, but I would recommend at least $150 a month, per unit, after all other anticipatable expenses, in order to give you some cushion.

The Risks of Overpaying Slightly

As Trammell Crow, the greatest single property owner in the U.S., is reported to have said, "Time heals all mistakes."

Even if you purchase a rental for slightly too much, such that it doesn't quite make enough income in the first few years, the natural inflation in rents, the natural increase in property values, and the fact that a fixed rate mortgage will not go up, will mean that even early mistakes get corrected over time. I bought such a property from a national bank as a foreclosure back in 2008. My first few years I held it, it was a dog. Essentially, I paid the same money I received in rents back to the bank, which had lent me the money to purchase the property I bought from it.

Nonetheless, today I make a healthy return on this property on a monthly cash flow basis and, of course, the real estate values have increased significantly as well. But the value again doesn't serve as a primary motivator; it's really about the monthly cash flow. I love to collect checks in the mail each month, while being a good landlord to my tenants there. This is a property where the tenant living with me, in 2017, is still the same individual who was my first renter in the property, in 2008.

Avoid Alligators

Now, I want to give you a strong note of caution. Overpaying for a property itself isn't necessarily a problem. A problem arises when you pay an amount for a property, or even if you get a great price on a property, but have financing and lease rates such that the cash flows you get from the property do not allow you to service the debt and maintenance costs.

That is what is called an alligator property: a property that eats away at you rather than feeding you. I was helping a friend purchase his first investment property, and he had listened to a video on YouTube that said that all the money is made at the time of buying. That is very true, especially for a flip. When purchasing a property to fix up quickly and resell quickly, it has to be purchased at a good price.

If you are in this business for the *long haul,* like me, it is somewhat different. For example, my view is that properties are for life: properties to send me checks in the mail, every month, for the rest of my life. I love that those checks are indexed for inflation, and my rents have always risen far faster than inflation.

Speculation on Appreciation

"Successful investing takes time, discipline, and patience. No matter how great the talent or effort, some things just take time: you can't produce a baby in one month by getting nine women pregnant."
Warren Buffett

I love housing. I love being in housing for the long-term. I want to give a word of warning against speculators who really don't care about housing, and just think that real estate is the way to fast money. Yes, it can be, and there are enough late night infomercials that provide real life examples of people who made a fast buck.

"Do what you love, and the money will follow."
Marsha Sinetar

Yes, I've made a medium fast buck in real estate too. However, I feel I was able to make that buck because I wasn't planning on it; I was intending on a long-term investment but ended up seizing an opportunity to sell it at a healthy profit rather than keep it.

Exit Strategies

"If plan A fails, remember there are 25 more letters."
Chris Guillebeau

This leads me to a discussion about exit strategies. In life, we ought to have contingency plans. This means that if our main plan, Plan A, doesn't work out, we have a Plan B and Plan C. An example is that you might target doing a long-term rental with a year or longer lease. Yet if for some reason it proves difficult to attract a long-term tenant at the price you are looking for to pay the mortgage and insurance and taxes and make a reasonable profit, you might try doing a solution like Airbnb.

This would increase your cash flow but, since this strategy requires a lot more hands-on management, the extra cash flow Airbnb offers shouldn't be considered gravy. Or you might furnish the rental unit and do medium term corporate housing, such as renting to contract workers who are doing a project in your city but actually reside elsewhere. They require furniture, TV, cable, and so forth; yet they might be your tenants for several months, rather than just days, like with Airbnb.

Reluctant Landlords

Occasionally, we see house flippers become reluctant landlords. They spent a lot of money renovating a property but can't sell at the price they need. They decide to rent the unit for a while until values catch up. Personally, I don't like this strategy. One of the appeals of purchasing a flip is that everything is brand new. The carpet has barely been walked on, the cabinets are brand new, and the tub, tile, and everything else is unblemished.

When you have tenants for a year or two, unless they are exceptionally meticulous in their care for the home, that brand new feeling may no longer remain. To get back to that pristine feel, you will likely end up wanting to re-install new carpet, repaint many of the walls, and possibly do things like replace faucets if they were cleaned in a way that scratched or otherwise marred their finish.

In a rental unit, none of the normal tenant wear and tear is a significant issue; however, going from a rental back to a pristine flip, an owner-occupant would not find any minor dings and evidence of having been lived in. This is challenging, and may take a little more investment before listing the place for sale at top dollar. See my other subchapter on letting go of perfectionism in the case of rentals.

Flips can require a different mindset than rentals in order to really command the highest returns. I often see advertisements by wholesalers—people who find discounted real estate and resell it without doing any work on it—stating things such as, "rehab for rental, $7K; rehab for flip, $25K."

Recurring Cases of Speculation Going Wrong

> *"Speculation is most dangerous when it looks easiest."*
> Warren Buffett

I see people who believe in *fast cash,* and are willing to violate the rules of sound investing to chase that pipe dream. They are willing to purchase an alligator property, which is a property that loses money on the monthly rent, hoping that, in two or three years, the property will have greatly increased in value, allowing for a quick sale at a profit of (pick a number), maybe, $150,000, or even $300,000.

While there are some lucky risk takers who tried this and succeeded, there are also many who tried and failed. I remember the people who bought preconstruction condos in Miami just before the bottom fell out of the condo market. In googling this to refresh my memory, I came across headlines that this exact phenomenon is happening again as I write this in 2017, with enough google results about this that the prior phase of this, which happened in 2007–2008, is no longer on the first few google pages. Here is a quote from a 2017 article:

"The lure: Buy a preconstruction condo from a developer in the early stages of development. The initial deposit is small and, in a booming market, the payoff big.... Everyone is in nirvana. This bet has been hot in the condo construction boom around the country. But in Miami, the bet is now collapsing. And preconstruction condo flippers, the lucky ones that could sell their units at all, are bathing in a sea of red ink."

(http://wolfstreet.com/2017/01/29/condo-speculation-collapses-in-miami-dade-condo-glut/ accessed July 23, 2017)

Here is the same, identical scenario from 2007: "As dozens of condominium towers conceived during Florida's real estate boom near completion, investors who snatched up units in the preconstruction phase in hopes of turning a quick profit are increasingly trying to break contracts, even walking away from fat deposits.

Motivated sellers are flooding online forums like Craigslist with advertisements for condo units, still months or years from being finished. And lawyers have been inundated with calls from people hoping to avoid closing on units they bought during the speculative craze of 2004 and 2005."
(http://www.nytimes.com/2007/05/26/us/26condo.html accessed July 23, 2017)

The Greater Fool Theory to Speculation

*"The individual investor should act consistently
as an investor and not as a speculator."*
Ben Graham

In my mind, any investment strategy that relies on the *greater fool theory* is innately flawed. This is the theory that I might overpay for a piece of property but, in 6 months or a year, I will find an even bigger fool, who will overpay even more than I did. If I am relying on a sale to be financially OK, and if I am already sensing that things are overpriced but hope that there are enough *fools* in the marketplace to continue the upward momentum of prices, I might not be well positioned for dealing with a minor easing up of real estate values or a glut in the supply of competing condos (or whatever the asset du jour is). That is the recipe for failure.

Like any boom and bust—from tulips in the 1700s to Beanie Babies—certain types of assets went from an undersupply to a glut, and a radical rethinking in the marketplace of what the true value of such an item was. If a thousand, or tens of thousands of people in your metropolitan area get the same idea about a hot trend, and then, all of a sudden, enough of them at the same time get tired of some negative aspect of the craze that was overlooked in the initial euphoria, you will have a recession for that asset.

If that craze involves a segment of real estate like condos, or even houses, there is a lot of money at stake. Many people will be looking to sell their asset at the same time. This allows the pool of available buyers to play sellers against each other and push down prices. Also, the most motivated sellers who want to unload quickly, because of financial pressures or because of fears that prices might plummet further, push the prices down. The dreamed of, speculative profits that people envisioned won't happen. Moreover, most of these people tend to think like speculators rather than true investors.

An investor is in the market for the long haul, and is willing to do the work that is required, such as leasing the property and taking on the property management chores that come with the territory. Speculators often throw their hands up when real work is required, and would rather walk away from real gains that are achievable in a few short years as asset values recover with the next cycle, rather than get their hands dirty doing something as unsavory as real work to earn the profits they had been envisioning.

Speculation is not the road to wealth. In fact, rarely is greed ever the road to wealth. My encouragement is for those of us who are serious about creating a real stream of income and appreciation to take genuine satisfaction in providing high-quality housing to people who cannot afford to own, or who aren't ready to own.

I love buying property for that sense of security. Whatever happens, I have one or more pieces of real estate where I could live, that I could liquidate if I absolutely had to, where I have security in the form of ownership of something very complete and tangible, that cannot be stolen, that cannot be totaled in a car crash, and that always provides enduring value to our species as humans.

Getting Kids into Real Estate

> *"I believe in giving my kids enough so they can do anything,*
> *but not so much that they can do nothing."*
> Warren Buffett

I have a dream about my son, when he is 16 and wants to earn his first car. He is now 12. I envision that he is willing and motivated to learn how to paint, to fix plumbing issues, to troubleshoot electrical items, to identify and fix things wrong with the roof or a furnace or water heater. Most importantly, I envision that he will be a better man, a better future husband, and a better member of society because of that.

Being a Landlord with Heart

I love the movie called *Mongol*. It's a great story of the Mongolian emperor, Genghis Khan. He revolutionizes Mongolian society by sharing a significantly larger percentage of the spoils with those who fight on his side. This gains him many loyal adherents. I liken this principle to the tenants I treat more compassionately than the apartment complexes, who early on the third day of the month hang 3-day notices warning tenants of an impending eviction filing if they don't pay asap. I understand that my tenants have problems in their lives, from aging parents to car accidents. I don't always like it, but I put up with some of the excuses they give me. Usually, this pays off, although it hasn't always.

Regardless, I'm proud to say that a large number of my tenants say that I'm the best landlord they've ever had. In one case, and I'm not recommending you do this, I allowed a family that had a baby on the way to get five months behind on their rent. This was a significant amount, which grew to more than $3,000. It got to the point where I finally talked to the family about moving out. Because of my conversation, where I just felt I couldn't wait any longer for more promises, they had already moved out a large couch that was very difficult to get in and out through a narrow basement entryway.

Somehow, they got access to funds through the mom getting student loans. They applied a chunk of the student loan to the past due rent. Even though they never moved that couch back in, they lived with me for three or four more years after that point before finally moving out of state.

Once again, I'm not recommending that you be this overly compassionate of a landlord. It is easy to get upside down and to not get your money that you are owed. However, by being a landlord, you are in a position to be a light in this world. You are able to use your best judgement and intuition to help deserving people when nobody else will. Most importantly, you're also in a position to help yourself, and be courageous and self-loving, by standing up for yourself and making sure that you are paid what you are owed by people who may not always fully understand that.

Over time, I have come to really believe that the journey towards prosperity is a journey of spiritual growth. Yes, there are also drug lords and corrupt politicians who amass extreme amounts of wealth. However, I think these are a minority, and their wealth is transitory and hollow. For example, I read in the *Wall Street Journal* that sales of luxury brands decreased because the Chinese government launched an anti-corruption drive.

(https://www.wsj.com/articles/luxury-goods-are-selling-again-on-chinese-smartphones-1500025322).

I prefer the alternative of wealth through integrity.

Doing Well Through Doing Good

I look at wealthy individuals who I admire and emulate: people like Bob, or Andrew Carnegie who started numerous public libraries in the US and around the world, or the founders of Chipotle, who provide a huge burrito and massive value in terms of healthy, ecologically conscious food. These people serve as proof that doing good allows us to do well. I am convinced that this model of ethical prosperity works, and I espouse it for myself and for you.

If I want to do well, it comes through being reputable and honest. Most importantly, it comes through being the person people line up to do business with.

I see this at some of my open houses. I intentionally structure my leases to be 18 or 24 months so that I have less of that interval between tenants, where I need to repaint, maybe re-carpet, and lose a little bit of rent. In exchange for that, I offer very competitive rent prices and make sure my tenants know that they benefit from locked in rental prices, when in the next year, most other landlords' rents would be going up.

I arrived three minutes late to one open house. There were about 30 people milling around on the lawn in front of the property. Of course, the property was rented in just one showing. I was joking with some of the applicants that next time I should hire a budding DJ to provide live entertainment and gain name recognition; there were so many people wanting to rent one studio apartment. That is the power of reputation, fairness, and offering value. Rip-off artists don't get this; when they make money, they rarely keep it.

Setting the Record Straight – Clogged Toilets at Midnight

There is a lot of misinformation about landlording. I've heard some of it, and it can sound intimidating, even to me as a veteran, until I think about how rarely some of the horror stories have happened to me, and how rarely so called horror stories were actually challenging to handle.

There is a famous line used in a few seminars I've attended. It's about never-ending calls by tenants saying the toilet is clogged, and they need it fixed at midnight on New Year's Eve. In my 500-tenant years of landlording, I've never gotten that call.

Yes, it's true. Your mutual fund manager will never call you at midnight telling you his toilet is clogged and asking you to fix it. Partially, that's because he lives in a mansion that he funds with your money.

But what would I do if I did get that type of call? I would leave a message for my local rooter company to contact my tenant at the phone number I provide on the voicemail, and I would ask them to contact me as soon as they re-open for business. If I was really nervous about a timely response, I might leave the same message for a second company and say that it's urgent, that I also contacted another company, and that whichever company contacts me first with a prompt appointment to address the issue, gets the business.

When we treat our tenants well, they reciprocate. People have basic needs, and I acknowledge that, and I empathize with their plight whenever it is brought to my attention. At the same time, we all have to be reasonable. Plumbers are typically not waiting for the next drain to clog at midnight on New Year's Eve. Business will open when it opens, and the issue will be solved as soon as possible.

Because I am firm when I need to be but nice to everyone I do business with, trades people put me ahead of their less popular clients. Mainly, I pay promptly and I'm good to work with. For the same reasons that I'm nice yet firm when I need to be, my tenants understand the inevitable things that happen. If they were a homeowner, they would have the same deal.

A Screw-Up Can Actually Make Your Tenants Like You More

In service marketing, there's the concept of service recovery. The scenario is that a business screws up for the customer, and then does an amazing job fixing their mistake. When the business puts effort into addressing the issue, the customer is usually more surprised, more delighted with the business, more likely to be a repeat customer, and more likely to recommend the business to others.

Ultimately, good handling of a minor disaster can have a more positive effect on customer satisfaction than if the business had just done a decent job up front, with no special cause for making the transaction memorable.

In that spirit, in the case that my tenants really put up with a massive inconvenience, I'll buy them a box of chocolates and some flowers, or maybe a gift card. One of the big techniques for increasing happiness is gratitude. When I'm grateful to my tenants, they are happier and, because I have happier tenants, I am happier. I enjoy thanking people. I'm not sure how, but when I do go out of my way to thank them, people create even more opportunities where I get to say a sincere thank you.

Learning to Be Gifted at Amazing Interactions with the People We Encounter

My friend, Stacy, is a superhero at this. She has a gift for recognizing amazingness in all the people she interacts with, and genuinely and sincerely expresses it. She gets more free desserts and other amazing favors than any person I've ever met. And it's not a self-serving thing; the people she interacts with genuinely love her and feel so brightened up by how Stacey is genuinely appreciative of their humanity and uniqueness. This applies to virtually anyone: the people who bring her food and serve her coffee, or those who fix her home or car, or decorate her amazing backyard, or whatever it is.

This notion of practicing appreciation, gratitude, and a genuine recognition of the human we are interacting with isn't a concept that only works with landlording; we can apply it in the office, at the grocery store, at restaurants, and with the car mechanic.

Chapter 4

Which Type of Property to Buy?

"The major fortunes in America have been made in land."
John D. Rockefeller

"The best investment on earth is earth."
Louis Glickman

"You don't need to be a rocket scientist. Investing is not a game where the guy with the 160 IQ beats the guy with the 130 IQ."
Warren Buffett

"...One dad had a habit of saying, 'I can't afford it.' The other dad forbade those words to be used. He insisted I ask, 'How can I afford it?' One is a statement, and the other is a question. One lets you off the hook, and the other forces you to think."
Robert Kiyosaki, Author of *"Rich Dad, Poor Dad"*

Types of Properties

There is a wealth of different categories of income-producing real estate you could invest in. These include condos, town homes, or single-family houses—both attached single-family houses, such as row houses, or detached single-family houses, such as the traditional house surrounded by a yard. Then there are small multi-family buildings, typically called duplexes, triplexes, and fourplexes, or quadplexes. Next, we start getting into the realm of commercial real estate. These are five or more unit multi-family residential buildings, retirement homes, self-storage complexes, mobile home parks, hotels and motels, casinos, strip malls, commercial, retail, industrial, and warehouse buildings. Then there may be investment opportunities in real estate through securitized options like REITS (Real Estate Investment Trusts), or more informal partnerships with people you may have connected with to invest in larger real estate deals.

I would not recommend getting too caught up on the various forms of real estate available. What this book primarily discusses is how to buy single-family residential real estate, which ranges from a condo or townhome to an attached or detached single-family home, although the core principles can apply to many other types of properties as well.

My personal recommendation, starting off as a first-time state investor, is to go with the least risky form of real estate that you can find a good deal on.

Why I Started Buying Condos as My Early Investments

Personally, I started buying condos. I liked the fact that a homeowners association, in exchange for a monthly fee, takes responsibility for the entire exterior of the building, which includes siding, roof, yard, trash, snow removal, parking facilities, and possibly even a pool and recreation room, a party/meeting room, and laundry facilities.
Often, HOA dues also include water and heat in their homeowners' association bills. The main point is that the maintenance of water piping, the heating system, any elevators, and the pool or other amenities the condo building may have, are typically covered by the HOA. Consequently, all I needed to worry about was paying my monthly homeowners dues by the due date, and taking care of the interior of my unit.

Not all Condo Associations are Perfect

"To demand perfection is a sure way to be disappointed in everybody, for you will be bound to think ill of others."
Monica Fairview

Later, as I became more experienced after remodeling several condos and understanding how to work with contractors and knowing what typical items cost, I started getting somewhat critical of certain homeowners' associations. I noticed in the less well run HOAs, that the all-volunteer HOA board did not do good due diligence or price comparison before selecting contractors. Sometimes the person hired by the HOA to do onsite management wasn't fully committed to keeping costs down for the HOA. Sometimes board members were hired to do work at prices that didn't reflect fair market value.

A quote I read in the minutes from an HOA board regarding this was, "There might be the appearance of impropriety, but it is only an appearance; there is no impropriety." This does not mean that all HOAs are bad. It simply means that you should do your homework, speak to the HOA president and more than one homeowner before committing to join a Homeowners' Association by purchasing a unit there.

One of the more extreme examples of an HOA overpaying for a service is a condo building where I used to own. The HOA paid $1,600 to have carpeted elevator floors replaced with linoleum. This was to solve the problem of residents mistakenly spilling bleach on the carpet as they were taking the elevator to the basement laundry room. At roughly $240 a square yard for linoleum, somebody made an inordinate amount of profit on that job. True, it's only $16 out of every owner's dues for that month, but money must be managed well, not squandered.

Success Stories of Normal People Investing in Condos

Eventually, I branched out into houses and multi-family properties to the point where I now only buy condos when I find an exceptional deal. Yet having owned a half-dozen condos, I remain grateful. Condos were the foundation of my real estate evolution; and I certainly wasn't the only one to do pretty well in condos. I met a bus driver named Dave, who was able to retire early, and prosperously, based on owning a portfolio of condos in the downtown Denver area.

A loan officer told me about another example of a long-haul truck driver who also bought a good number of condos, to the point where he was able to stop his long haul job and take on part time gigs while still having a very comfortable income.

To me, that is an example of how "normal" people can get into real estate investing, without needing to be overly *hands-on,* and can do very nicely for themselves. I intentionally put normal in quotes, because these individuals are different. They read books like this one but, even more importantly, they take action.

They spent their free time looking for deals, going out and touring them, making offers, lining up financing, managing the process of getting the units rented, and making sure the rent payment came in every month. When you do it right, it's easier than you think. This book is designed to give you the education you need to succeed!

Comparing Condos to Houses

One thing to evaluate when considering condos versus houses is to compare what the condo association dues are relative to if you made that same payment as a loan payment. How much extra house could you buy if the HOA dues went to the mortgage payment instead? For example, if HOA monthly dues are $250, then that is equivalent to being able to finance an extra $46,570.40, if you applied the same $250 to a 30-year fixed rate loan at 5%.

However, it's important to not mix apples and oranges; some of the HOA dues cover expenses you would need to cover yourself in a single-family property, including water, heat, exterior maintenance and repairs, and the like. Therefore, accounting for such items, it wouldn't be realistic to allocate the full $250 to just the loan. You would want to consider the full package, which includes the fact that a house with more privacy can command higher rents compared to the typical condo, where there are stricter noise rules and less freedoms about what you do, with whom, and at what time of night.

You can get a pretty good idea which way to lean by looking at the *for rent* ads on Craigslist, or Zillow or Trulia, or other *for rent* websites. Compare houses and condos, similar to the ones you see available for rent, to see how your financial numbers might stack up. Every market can be somewhat different and, therefore, providing you with generalizations will not help you reach conclusions that truly fit for your specific market and budget.

What Level of Fix-Up to Contemplate in Your First Rental Property

"Opportunity is missed by most people because it is dressed in overalls and looks like work."
Thomas Edison

I've helped various friends purchase their first rental property, and I see a wide variety of willingness to engage in repairs and renovations. Your comfort level might range anywhere along the spectrum from wanting to do no work at all, to being willing to tackle painting items yourself, to being willing to attempt tiling, grouting, and installing laminate or hardwood floors.

There really is no formula for who likes what. I have seen women, with no prior experience, tackle tearing apart their old bathroom with blue tub, tile, and toilet, and retiling the entire tub surround, as well as sanding and refinishing old wood floors. On the other hand, I have seen men who have no problem admitting that doing any such work is simply not their cup of tea. There is no right or wrong. It's important to be aware of your strengths and desires, and to not deviate from the path that brings you the most joy.

I started off doing landscaping after college, and I learned about construction as I went along. One job, on which I learned so much, was building a 5-car garage for a CEO of a bank. The 1200 square foot garage was a scaled down replica of the house and, while working on it, our crew used to joke that, with some plumbing, this *garage* would make a delightful house. This experience propelled me into building my own home.

The Amazing Things We Can Learn with the Right Resources

My experience, as a man with a background in landscape construction, was that reading the *how to build a house* books, written by men, for men, seemed to skip steps. I couldn't comprehend how to fully do key tasks. For example, step three would be X, and step four would be Z; I could not figure out why step Y was not explained. So, I was jubilant when I found a very well described book—something along the lines of *Home Building for Women*—whose exact title I no longer remember and can't seem to find, since the book was published somewhere between the 1960s and 1990s.

This library book helped me bridge those gaps. As a young man, I used to keep the book upside down in my old Ford Tempo that I used to haul building materials up to my property because, at that stage of my life, I found it mildly embarrassing that I was reading books seemingly exclusively *for women*, as if men should be born with the innate knowledge that I somehow lacked. But, with this book, I was able to get the job done.

What made me take on building my own house versus just purchasing a condo when I moved back to Colorado? I had a limited amount of money: about $10,000 at the time. My thought process had been that putting in the sweat equity would give me a much greater financial return in the long-term.

Moreover, I knew that if I got started, I would have to finish. I was certain that when there is a will there is a way. I would find the ways to learn the skills to do all the tasks needed to build the house. The alternative for me was buying a completed condo. Yet I felt that doing so would continue my being afraid to fix things for fear of making things worse than they were before. I am that way when it comes to auto mechanics.

Acknowledging That Not All Things Are Our Cup of Tea

I have decided to limit the amount of work I do repairing my vehicles, no matter how much money people tell me I could save. It's just not my thing. I likely would have turned out thinking the same way about fixing houses, if I hadn't forced myself to jump in the deep end by committing to build a house from scratch.

That story could be a separate book in future; there are so many ridiculous and unpredictable mishaps, and so many rookie mistakes. Who builds a house where the door on the lower level, and the window on the level above, are misaligned by 8 inches? A rookie! Who fixes that mistake by building an elegant tower addition, with 180 degree views, in front of this misalignment? A rookie with passion. Nowadays, my typical new purchases require extensive remodeling. I'm passionate about fixing up houses and making them beautiful again, on a budget, because it is really something I consider my art and something I greatly enjoy doing; I view it as a hobby, and fun rather than work.

The average car is composed of 30,000 parts. To me, a car has an enormous amount of complexity. I would be terrified to work on things like brakes, and then realize that, because I made some beginner's mistake, I wasn't able to stop in time before running into a boulder or, even worse, a semi-truck filled with gasoline.

When I look at houses, unlike cars, they are built of non-complex materials. Moreover, houses don't move, unless they are in an earthquake zone during an earthquake, so we don't need the complexity of axles, shocks, transmissions, brakes, and the like.

Houses are made of 2 x 4s, big sheets of plywood, manufactured windows that are just simply screwed into place, a whole bunch of caulking that is used to hide all the defects that occur during construction, and materials like drywall and mud, paint, and carpet. The more complex items like electrical and plumbing can be left to the professionals; or I might get a detailed book on the matter, and watch YouTube videos to learn to do some of the more pedestrian elements of those trades by myself, such as switching out faucets, replacing lights, and installing ceiling fans.

I recently taught myself to do a passable job at installing carpet by watching three or four YouTube videos on the topic. The overall lesson I am trying to convey is that we are all capable of learning many things, and the best way to do it is to allow yourself time to grow. You may consider yourself to be all thumbs. I essentially consider myself rather unskilled and unsuited when it comes to car maintenance. Yet when it comes to working on houses, I believe I am a rock star. Because of that attitude, I enjoy what I do, and the work I do is something I'm extremely proud of, even if there are skilled professionals who might point out certain things that they would have done differently.

How Our Mindset Shapes Our Ability to Learn

"Stop being afraid of what could go wrong,
and start being excited of what could go right."
Tony Robbins

On the topic of learning things we never thought we might be good at, or never even considered tackling, a great book I recommend is *Mindset: The New Psychology of Success,* by Carol S. Dweck. What this books affirms is something that I have found to be true in my own life: If we are willing to put in the effort and accept the fact that just because we don't currently have skills, and that by putting in effort and facing our fear of failing, and our fear of not being perfect on our first try, we can teach ourselves more than we ever believed possible.

A key component is accepting that we aren't great, or even good yet, and that we can become better if we apply ourselves. Most importantly, nothing we do reflects on our inborn greatness. The only thing that truly reflects our greatness is our willingness to learn more. The book gives inspiring examples, such as the real life story that inspired the movie *Stand and Deliver*, where teacher, Jaime Escalante, teaches inner city youth college level calculus. I also must commend my own mother as an example.

In our house, while I was growing up, my mom did most of the handiwork that needed to be done. I learned from her that if we try, we can often do exceptional things. It has nothing to do with gender or the amount of knowledge we start with. It has to do with wanting to achieve an outcome and being willing to risk failure in the pursuit of doing so—and my mom never failed. Yes, I never saw a varnished pine kitchen countertop outside of our house where I grew up in Cape Town, South Africa, but it was a completely satisfactory countertop, and it served its purpose.

You Might Just Be as Good as that Pro You Were Going to Hire

It's also worth noting that a hurried pro, who is rushing to their next job, will at times not take the care and time that you would to do the job; so, his skill, balanced against your lesser skill but greater care, might create equivalent results. Again, like all of life, this is a balancing act. You must balance your time, the availability of tools and know-how, and whether the price you're getting on a house that needs work justifies paying somebody to do the work, or purchasing the tools and materials and making the time to do the work yourself. We all have 24 hours a day. Our level of success is shaped by how we utilize that time.

One more note on working on houses versus cars: I knew of a guy who spent 4 years restoring a Ford Pinto. He spent hundreds of hours and thousands of dollars on parts. In the end, he had something that looked like an almost new Pinto. In the same amount of time, I remodeled a couple of houses. I created tens, if not hundreds, of thousands of dollars' worth of *sweat equity* in the time he created a car that's still only worth less than $20,000.

It is almost certain that the Ford Pinto did not gain enough value to offset the time and expense invested in it. In the case of my houses, my time and expenses were amply rewarded in the marketplace. Yes, it might be easier to buy a used Pinto, but why play small? The results are there for those of us who seize the initiative to play BIG! Read on to learn how.

> *"As long as you are going to be thinking anyway, think big."*
> Donald Trump

Would You Live in Your Rental Unit?

A lot of new landlords decide that they will only purchase and rent property where they would live as well. I did the same. I bought my first piece of land at age 21, with the intention of building a house there, and my first rental, a condo, at the age 25, with the intention that I would happily live there. In fact, after my divorce, that came to pass; I ended up living there for almost a year.

Yet, as I have matured as a landlord, I came to realize that purchasing, fixing, and renting properties where I would never live, at rents that match an income level I would never be content at getting by with, is also a service to members of the community who need housing that I personally would not be content with.

The main reason to pursue purchasing a property that you would live in is that it creates a pool of renters that match you. We are well suited to evaluating people similar to us. We work with people like us, have neighbors like us, and hang out with people like us. When going far in either direction, up or down, we're out of our element and less able to operate with full experience and intuition, and all the benefits these provide. Properties we would live in, with tenants who are at a level of society we are familiar interacting with, is a great place to start.

That said, during a particularly challenging phase of my divorce, I slept on a sleeping bag at a property where much of the subfloor (the level floor you walk on, underneath the finished flooring, such as carpet or wood floor) was missing. I had to step carefully to avoid dropping through the floor joists to the dirt floor in the crawlspace underneath (and possibly emasculating myself). That is a property that was not rent ready at all, and that even the most brazen slumlord should not have been willing to risk renting as-is, in its lawsuit-inviting condition. What that proves is that there is always a need for housing. When someone is going through a rough time, they will accept, and even be grateful for, shelter that is less glamorous than what they might be aiming for. Next, the market is far bigger for a bread and butter, lower income rental than it is for exclusive, luxury penthouses, where monthly rent is several times monthly minimum wage income. Having a bigger market means more demand, more competition, and less vacancy for your rental.

Chapter 5

Find a Broker, Get Listings, and Tour Properties

"Don't wait to buy real estate. Buy real estate and wait."
Will Rogers

*"Now, one thing I tell everyone is learn about real estate.
Repeat after me: real estate provides the highest returns,
the greatest values, and the least risk."*
Armstrong Williams, TV and radio host

*"Opportunities will come and go,
but if you do nothing about them, so will you."*
Richie Norton

*"There comes a moment in every life when the Universe presents
you with an opportunity to rise to your potential. An open door that
only requires the heart to walk through, seize it and hang on. The
choice is never simple. It's never easy. It's not supposed to be. But
those who travel this path have always looked back and realized
that the test was always about the heart. ...The rest is just practice."*
Jaime Buckley

I wrote earlier about how I found Gina and she was my agent for a large number of transactions. I only found Gina after working with a pair of agents who I considered pushy and unethical.

I fully encourage you to find the best agent possible. If someone isn't meeting your needs, or is more concerned with their commission than your real estate success, they are probably not the right agent for you. Be willing to say that out loud and move on to find a good agent. This goes with my earlier comment about the journey of wealth being a spiritual journey. Part of this journey is banishing people from our inner circle if they are not aligned with our highest good. If these people block us from gaining our best, they also block us from giving our best to the rest of the world.

I see it too often: a budding investor understands that real estate is the road to wealth. They somehow team up with an agent who's more concerned about a single commission than creating a long-term relationship, and long-term real estate success for that client. They push their client into purchasing a property that is not ideal as a rental. That client bites their teeth out on this first investment property, and later decides to give it up, selling the property and exiting the business. That is really unfortunate and, I believe, the real estate agent is often partially to blame for the challenges their client encounters.

Not every property listed for sale is a great investment property, and a good agent is patient enough to allow you the time to find the right one rather than insisting that you jump on one of the first 10 or 20 properties that you are shown.

A great way to familiarize yourself with the market, and with the availability of different properties in different neighborhoods, is to ask your agent to send you auto emails daily from the multi-list service, or MLS.

My Morning Ritual of Browsing Properties

I used to wake up and, first thing, go to my computer to look at any listings that were listed for sale that previous day. Out of necessity, during the *heyday* of bank-owned properties during the real estate recession, I would instruct my agent to write offers purely on having seen the listing from her emails. This was imperative because, if I didn't, by 10 a.m. that property would be under contract. I'm not advocating you do this *sight unseen offer strategy* for your first deal, but I am advocating that you look at properties daily, before other investors get the best deals, and that you're willing to make the time to rush to look at a property that is clearly exceptionally well-priced, and write an offer.

If you won't, somebody else will.

Seizing Opportunity

As Tony Robbins says, "The opportunity of a lifetime comes along every two weeks." However, that does not mean that the opportunity of a lifetime stands still in front of you waiting for you to grab it. It comes and, if you blink and stop to rub your eyes, it might keep going. My website has a good deal analysis spreadsheet you could use to evaluate your first property. A spreadsheet like that is very helpful and allows you to do scenario analysis on different loan options and different rents based on the level of finish that the property has. However, I also want you to learn to be prepared to make snap judgments about whether a property is a good deal or not.

The basic rule of thumb that I use is that if I buy a property for $100,000, I should be able to get $1,000 per month in rent. Essentially, the monthly rent should be 1/100 of the purchase price. If I get that ratio, I'm happy. This, essentially, means that the property will pay for itself in 8 years and 4 months.

In many markets, it is very rare to find that type of ratio but, with currently low interest rates, that ratio is not necessary to achieve a good rental return. You may be in a position where you relax that ratio and say 110 times monthly rent is the purchase price, or possibly 120 times, if you qualify for a fixed rate loan at a great interest rate.

The key is that you've done enough spreadsheet analyses that you know what your rule of thumb quick analysis ratio should be. If you see a property in your morning perusal of the MLS listings that your agent sends you that matches those ratios, you should call and tell your work that you're running a little bit late; go see it first so that you can promptly write an offer. You may benefit from getting your agent to trust you and be willing to work with you to gain access to properties even if your agent can't always attend the showing in person.

It is always better to make a strong offer based on actually having seen the property. Even with all the amazing information we have available online, cameras cannot give you a true perspective of what the real estate truly looks like. However, as you get more familiar with certain neighborhoods and certain types of property, you will find that many properties in the same area, built around the same time, of the same style, will be relatively consistent; your need to see every single property, especially if it was built more recently, before making an exceptionally urgent offer, will be reduced.

To recap, if you have done your research to the point where you see an amazing deal on a property that is quite similar to other properties you have seen before, do not risk losing out. Be decisive—juggle your ability to see the property with the need to write an offer quickly and make a decision that positions you to be the buyer who actually gets to own that amazing deal.

Tour Properties

"The difference between something good and
something great is attention to detail."
Charles R. Swindoll

"It's the little details that are vital.
Little things make big things happen."
John Wooden

When you tour income properties you are considering buying, there are a number of important factors to pay attention to. I detail these key ones here, but I want to address the most important one up front. This is your intuition. If that feels off, beware. If it feels right, still be aware, but listen to that inner voice of yours.

Curb Appeal

The way the curb appeal strikes you is similar to the way it will strike prospective tenants. Look for things like the character of the neighborhood, the general feeling of safety, of lighting, the availability of parking, landscaping, trees and vegetation, the other homes on the street, as well as the level of overall maintenance in that municipality.

Location

Many agents will tell you that for residential real estate, being located on a busy street is bad, and lowers value. I don't necessarily agree with that for many types of rental properties. A simple *for rent* sign on a busy street can get you a lot of eyeballs and phone calls, and an easy way to fill the vacancy. Yes, it's true that if you, yourself, have small children, you might not want to live there, but for many tenants, who don't have children, it's often an excellent location. A busy street can be closer to public transport, and closer to shopping or restaurants and nightlife. This is a factor that can get you a lower price on buying a property and, simultaneously, create a higher rental return because your marketing costs can be lower and your tenant retention better.

Interior Ambiance

> *"We are continually faced by great opportunities brilliantly disguised as insoluble problems."*
> Author Unknown

The interior is critical. Be very conscious of your reaction when you first open the door. How does the home strike you? Does it feel open and inviting? Is it closed and cramped? Can the feeling of the home be improved with the choice of different wall, ceiling, and flooring colors?

Be aware that a property that looks and feels awful when you enter, but where all the awfulness is created by poor taste of the seller, is a financial opportunity. A property with purple walls, a black ceiling, and orange shag carpet will scare away most buyers. A property that smells of cat piss, once again, might command a much lower price than is justified the cost of a few gallons of Kilz primer and new pad and carpet. That differential could be your gain. As one investor said, "If you smell pet urine, inhale deeply. That is the smell of money."

Is the Layout Suitable for Your Target Renter?

For example, do guests have to access the bathroom by going through your tenants' bedroom? Is there more than one bathroom so that if there was a clogged toilet, the tenants would have a second bathroom, and there would be less urgency to deal with the issue? Is there room for a dining room table? Is the bedroom large enough for a bed and to still close the door? This is often a problem in Victorian houses, where bedrooms didn't get the square footage they now do.

Views

What are the views like? I used to live in the mountains and had a great view of beautiful snowcapped mountains. I always wondered about some of my neighbors who had a view of basically nothing but trees. What were they doing living in the mountains if they couldn't enjoy a nice view? Unless you get a significant discount on a property that is in a location that probably should have good views and doesn't, you might want to consider that in your equation. Gorgeous views make an excellent picture to include in your rental advertisement; the lack thereof is sure to be commented on by your tenant applicants.

Safety and Security

What is the security like? Does the neighborhood feel safe? Is the parking lot well lit, and does the same apply to the street? In marginal cases, just because it might not be the ideal location you or your significant other would choose to live in, does not mean that it makes a bad rental location.

Neighborhood

> *"In investing, what is comfortable is rarely profitable."*
> Robert Arnott

I have found that the nicer neighborhoods often have lower rental returns than the more marginal ones. Then again, I operate in Denver where there are no truly bad neighborhoods, I may not be familiar with some of the more *ghetto* neighborhoods that do exist elsewhere. I still advise reasonable caution and a level of comfort in whatever neighborhood you choose to invest in.

Generally, marginal properties can be bought at a lower price and at a higher ratio of rent to purchase price. Once again, everything is a balancing act, and for taking on a little more risk and being willing to spend time in neighborhoods that you might not choose to live in, better returns can be earned than is common in the nice neighborhoods where you wouldn't have a second thought.

An example for my local area is Boulder, Colorado, vs Denver. In Boulder, it's not uncommon to get a very low ratio of rent to purchase price. For example, a $500,000 property in Boulder may only rent for $2,500. This would not even be enough to cover a mortgage if you were looking to purchase a property like that today. At the same time, in Denver, you might purchase a property for 180,000, and receive $1,500 in monthly rent. Why would you choose Boulder?

Yes, it's true: Denver has a higher crime rate, occasional gang shootings, government housing projects that are a hotbed of crime and which lower property values in the surrounding neighborhood, lots of potholes, and just a grittier, more urban feel, which can be both cool and a liability. At its heart, Denver is a great bet for rental returns that work. It's a delightful, cosmopolitan city and, as of late, the number one city for millennials to move to.

Parking

Parking is always an important consideration. Most of us have at least one car, and tenants that do have cars are often better positioned to have access to employment opportunities that pay more and offer greater flexibility. Parking has value, and you could charge extra for it, either to people who are not your residential tenants, or include it as part of the package as an element of your rental that creates value.
If you are renting to very low income tenants who cannot afford their own transportation, be aware that if there is any kind of shortfall, such as even a brief illness or disability, they might lose income and not be able to make rent for a period of time.

Major Building Components to Assess

There are a set of common building elements that you typically want to evaluate for their condition, unless you are in a Home Owners Association where some of these elements are not your responsibility. Nonetheless, I always recommend assessing how current and proactive an HOA is in terms of maintenance. As a completely unusual example that took me by complete surprise, I once showed a condo that was listed as, *HOA replacing common area carpet.* The carpet had been heavily stained with paint when the common area walls were repainted, without masking the carpet. I asked the agent, "How long has the HOA been planning to replace that carpet?" The agent answered, "Five years."

The building components to assess are:

- the foundation
- the roof
- windows
- plumbing (including water supply lines), typically galvanized, copper, or pex; drain piping; and the water heater
- heating systems, such as the furnace or boiler
- cooling systems, such as the AC or swamp cooler
- electrical system (also known as *the wiring*)

Foundation

Obviously, the foundation is a critical component of the structure. A problematic foundation can dramatically lower the value of your house. In Colorado, there are neighborhoods with *swelling soils,* such that if a foundation was not engineered to handle this, these soils would cause heaving of the property—after a dramatic change in moisture, residents might find doors jammed shut. Over time, numerous houses experience some sort of sagging, settling, or other unevenness. Often this can be remedied, but this requires engineering and tearing flooring and other items down to the structural components, so it is not for the faint of heart.

I find that for single-family houses, sometimes sellers will disclose structural issues when they aren't major, but other times, sellers will have serious structural issues that they tried to cover up and not disclose anything. In the first scenario, I am likely to get a good deal; in the second, there is a risk of overpaying.

I once toured an old Victorian house that clearly had some structural issues, but they didn't seem terribly severe, so I made an offer. During the inspection period, I got very suspicious about drywall having been put up along the north wall of the basement. I reached up and pulled on the drywall. The drywall ripped off the few screws that it had been held in place with, and an avalanche of bricks pushed the drywall toward and on top of me. When the dust had settled, and I had crawled out from underneath the drywall, I could see that the entire foundation wall had collapsed, and I was looking at the exterior dirt with roots woven along its flat surface.

I am not espousing tearing up walls or creating any type of damage during an inspection. However, I highly recommend being highly suspicious when you see inconsistencies that point to a cover-up, such as 3 unfinished basement walls, and one poorly finished one that looks out of place.

Roof

It's worth being aware of that replacing a roof does cost a fair sum of money, and that any time you identify a big ticket deferred maintenance item, you should expect the owner/seller to bear a portion, if not all of that cost. The same goes for replacing furnaces, windows, or other building elements that need to be addressed. Some mortgage lenders will make it a loan condition that key elements are handled to protect their collateral from degradation if you, for example, didn't have the money to make timely mortgage payments, and replace the roof.

It's also worth noting that for multi-family properties, some insurance carriers are more hesitant to ensure flat roof properties, even though a flat roof is a very typical roofing style for multi-family properties. This is especially relevant in states like Colorado where substantial hail damage is a yearly risk, and where premiums can rise much faster than inflation, to compensate.

Essentially, your goal is to assess items that are likely to create cost for you in the near future, identify them proactively, and get the seller to pay for them or credit you some amount of money against the purchase price to reflect your need to address these items in the near future.

Windows

Windows that are in bad condition, or that are old aluminum or steel, single-pane windows, can dramatically increase your heating bill. Moreover, nobody likes to live in a property where the wind whistles through shut windows, where you feel cold drafts, or where there is little muffling of exterior noise.

A common failure to watch out for with older, double-pane windows is condensation between the windows, which means that the seal between the windows has failed. This type of failed double-pane window loses insulation value.

The only remedy for fogged windows is replacement. Often, I find that the cost of replacing the pane is as much or more than just ordering and installing an entire new window, so I usually go with new windows, unless the old one is installed in such a way that it is hard to replace.

Plumbing

In the realm of plumbing, I recommend checking if any galvanized piping still exists. Look in the basement and under the kitchen and bathroom sinks for steel piping that often looks corroded. If galvanized piping remains in your home, it is likely very close to the end of life. Eventually, galvanized piping will spring pinhole leaks. Furthermore, accumulated internal corrosion will narrow the internal diameter of the pipe and clog your faucet strainers and shower heads, limiting the water pressure you experience.

If you do purchase a home with galvanized pipes (called *galvie* by plumbers), I would recommend a wholesale replacement of all galvanized piping with a new material, such as copper or pex. I love pex (cross-linked polyethylene). It has some substantial advantages over copper:

- PEX is significantly cheaper than copper (roughly a third the price of copper).
- PEX is faster to install than copper. The connections are faster to make and, since the tubing is flexible, you can run the piping significantly more easily than rigid straight copper allows. This reduces the labor costs of the repiping.
- PEX won't corrode like copper in areas where the water is acidic.
- While PEX may eventually break after several freeze/thaw cycles, PEX is less likely to fail catastrophically in the very first freeze/thaw cycle, the way copper piping will. The main failure point for PEX with freezes are the brass fittings and copper crimp rings.

Water Heaters

Extremely old water heaters should be replaced when you purchase a property. Ones that seem in good shape are often okay, as long as you are aware that this type of appliance can fail any time, with no advance warning, once the initial warranty (typically 3, 6, or 10 years, generally noted on the tank) has expired.

Water heaters can fail catastrophically; everything is fine until all of a sudden they blow a leak and start spraying water into whatever location they are located in. Recently, in a single-family house where the water heater was located in a very small basement area, I had a water heater fail. Since the tenants did not know how to turn off the water supply, the water heater kept leaking to the point where the small basement flooded to a level such that the furnace circuit board and blower motor were submerged under water. This caused a level of damage where it was more cost effective to purchase a new furnace than to swap out parts and hope for the best.

Hot water heaters are relatively inexpensive. Typically, they can be purchased for under $500, and some plumbers will install them for $300 or less. There are several types of water alarms that can alert you when the water heater first fails, when hopefully the amount of water leaking from the water heater is not yet a massive amount.

Heating

Furnaces can last a surprisingly long time, or can fail shortly after installation if they are subjected to stresses like being submerged under water. As a layperson, I am not well equipped to assess for the most worrisome flaw of furnaces—a cracked heat exchanger. This is when the combustion air from the furnace jets, which spew out flames, mixes with the breathing air that is being heated and recirculated thorough your home. The typical way of addressing a cracked heat exchanger is to purchase a new furnace. The heat exchanger is the whole upper part of the inside of the furnace; unhooking and reinstalling the furnace to access that is similar to replacing it from a labor cost perspective.

Cooling

I personally know very little about AC systems, since I operate in an area of the country where I consider them more optional than mandatory. A newer AC that works is probably fine. Older models are likely to be more failure prone, noisier, and less energy efficient.

Electrical Wiring

One item that is typically not that easy to identify without removing cover plates, but which a home inspector will typically evaluate, is whether the wiring is aluminum, which can be problematic and often justifies a somewhat lower purchase price.

A note on aluminum wiring: I own one or two properties that do have aluminum wiring. While I haven't gone to the lengths of ripping it out and replacing it, it is worth being aware that aluminum wiring may require extra care when hooking up outlets and fixtures. Some codes and some manufacturers of electrical components call for anti-oxidant compound that prevents oxidation between copper and aluminum wiring connections.

As stated by the *New York Times*, "unless certain safety procedures are undertaken, every outlet, light switch, and junction box connected to such circuits is a fire waiting to happen." "This is an area we feel very strongly about," said Scott Wolfson, a spokesman for the [Consumer Product Safety] commission. "Aluminum wiring in a house presents a very serious potential fire hazard."
http://www.nytimes.com/2006/02/19/realestate/the-fire-dangers-of-aluminum-wiring.html, accessed July 24, 2017.

Chapter 6

Offers, Inspections, and Closing

"Security is mostly a superstition.
Life is either a daring adventure or nothing."
Helen Keller

"It's not because things are difficult that we dare not venture.
It's because we dare not venture that they are difficult."
Seneca

"Pearls don't lie on the seashore.
If you want one, you must dive for it."
Chinese proverb

"What great thing would you attempt
if you knew you could not fail?"
Robert Schuller

Love vs. Finances

When you decide to make an offer, be aware of the dance between love or infatuation with a property, and the dispassionate evaluation of financial returns. Occasionally, an extraordinary piece of real estate makes you fall in love with it, even though the numbers don't work. It is worth remembering that if the finances don't work, you will eventually fall out of love with the property. On the other hand, if the property is far less attractive and appealing, but the numbers are great, which does not spark love in the near-term, you eventually grow to love the numbers, and the property and how it takes care of you financially.

How to Make a Strong Offer

> *"If I hadn't been fair, I would never have made*
> *the $6 billion in real estate deals that I did.*
> *I mean, if you're not fair, people don't want to deal with you."*
> Jerry Reinsdorf

As an investor, I want the seller to know that I am serious and committed. I am planning to build wealth, and that starts with having an excellent reputation. I am decisive and follow through. At the same time, I am behaving as a professional, and I have a plan to do due diligence to the appropriate level, in a manner that meets both my needs and the sellers.

One way to be sincere and fair to the seller is to eliminate any possible conflicts and reasons to not proceed with the sale as soon as possible. That way, the seller is not taking a property off the market for several weeks, only to be back at square one with the blemish of the property looking on the MLS like it has sat without moving, which creates a red flag and negative price pressure.

On the other hand, as a smart investor, if I see that red flag, without having created it myself, it is fair game to go in with an offer that reflects the truism that a property that is languishing on the market is typically overpriced. Explicitly having contractual clauses in the additional provisions that I am protecting the seller by accelerating inspections, title review, and similar due diligence, makes me a better buyer to deal with in a multiple offer scenario. This occurs commonly in a seller's market, where there is an imbalance between a larger number of buyers and smaller number of sellers, and where sellers can pick and choose between competing offers.

Another way to make a strong offer is to not just have a prequalification letter but also a pre-approval letter. A prequalification letter indicates, based on answering preliminary questions, I have been deemed as eligible for qualifying for a loan up to a certain amount. A preapproval is much more detailed. I have submitted my personal loan paperwork to allow a decision that I, as a borrower(s), am approved for a loan, and now just the property needs to pass the appraisal hurdle.

Being willing to make a high earnest money deposit is another way of being a very serious investor. I once bought an $111,000 property with a $100,000 earnest money deposit. This can be risky if something untoward happened where an earnest money dispute tied up my money for a length of time. In my case, the strategy worked: I was the most serious buyer, who was rewarded with having the winning offer that purchased the property.

Owning Entity

Many real estate workshops will teach you about the benefits of owning properties in the name of trusts, LLCs, and other types of entities that provide asset protection and anonymity. This is beyond the scope of this book to discuss in any detail, and there is much good advice that is well worth acquiring and implementing. Check my website, at www.RentalRealEstateBook.com, for more material around this.

However, as a beginning investor, if you are looking to buy a property, and finance it with a bank loan, the most expedient way to do so is to purchase the property in your own name, since that is what virtually all banks require when they extend you a loan. Most banks on your first investment property will not work with you on a business loan, and you may not yet have the know-how to structure things upfront. What many asset protection workshops will teach you is how to move properties from your personal name into the appropriate entity after closing, once you have gotten the loan in place. Many banks insist that you own the property at the time of signing the loan in your personal name, since they're extending credit to you as an individual and not to a corporate entity. Generally, with a business, especially with a loan that doesn't allow the bank personal recourse against you, their risk of non-repayment might be considered greater.

To recap, the advice here is to not let details, such as which entity you will ultimately own the property in, derail you from moving forward and acquiring your first property. I recommend taking bold, yet sufficiently informed action, and being ready to adjust as you go. Despite the horror stories people use to sell asset protection seminars—since, as we all know, fear sells— very rarely do the horror stories truly materialize. If they did, the press would be filled with more of them.

It Is like the old adage of the plane flying from New York to Hawaii. The plane is on course, on a direct path to Hawaii, maybe 1% of the time; the other 99% of the time, it is flying in the wrong direction. The only reason the plane arrives in the end is that it makes many little course corrections during the course of the flight to ultimately arrive at the destination. If a pilot were so fixated on being on course 100% of the time, he would have to sit on the runway in New York in paralysis and fear, because such perfection and efficiency is not possible.

As in the old Latin proverb, fortune rewards the bold; and you, dear reader, have what it takes to be bold, decisive, and to reap the rewards of your courage. This book is here to help!

Inspections

Inspection of your property is an item that can materially affect how well the transaction goes for you. If you are new as an investor, I highly recommend using the best home inspector that you can find. In my area, I found one company where the owner is a structural engineer. I used him several times and was very pleased with the quality of services. One time, I used another individual in his firm because the owner was not available. That individual missed a very key issue: the entire north wall of the structure had the wood framing rotted out to about knee high. The entire roof structure was resting on the brick veneer rather than on the structural stud framing that it had originally been built on.

An experienced and conscientious inspector is a great asset. You want someone who really is willing to get on his hands and knees in the darkest corners of the crawl space with a flashlight. You want an inspector who is willing to have you there, asking as many questions as you can come up with, and being willing to educate you so that, over time, you can get more confident about doing a similar level of inspection yourself.

Regarding my story about the rotten north wall, the cost to repair it, after some nail-biting and consulting with several experts, in the end was twenty 2x4 studs and a couple of $50 jack posts to lift the top wall plate up an inch or so. Nonetheless, there is the potential for things to have gotten much more costly, which is why using the most competent inspector, and being there at the same time so that he is not tempted to skip the dark corners of a crawlspace with lots of cobwebs, is a very wise idea. This is especially true in the very beginning of your investing career where you still have a lot to learn.

My fear of dealing with that rotted out north wall is also one of the reasons that I started buying condos early on. Once again, I recommend going with asset classes where you can succeed at a healthy level and learn until you get the level of comfort and familiarity to branch out into other types of assets. You will know whether you are ready for the properties where you may not be paying for a Home Owners Association (HOA) to shelter you from various types of risk, and where you might take on managing the risks of roof leaks and similar HOA handled issues for equivalent or less money than the typical HOA is able to.

Also, don't be afraid to insist on due diligence if you wonder that the inspector doesn't seem to be looking at certain items. I sold a condo once where the buyer also hired a licensed home inspector. There were a couple of minor nits the inspector could have found, but all she had documented in the inspection report was that the porch light didn't work. Clearly, that superficial level of thoroughness wasn't what I would want from my inspector if I was that buyer. Often, paying for a second $350 inspection with a truly qualified inspector is better than getting surprised later with an unanticipated bill that a competent inspector would have flagged.

Typically, in an inspection, the inspector will identify a long litany of items that need to be addressed. Even with items that are just fine, or even perfect, the inspector may label them as *serviceable* rather than simply stating good or even excellent. Many inspectors pride themselves on being extremely *analytical,* if you know the four letter version of that term, and will identify lots of issues that may or may not be truly an issue.

On a flip, I had one inspector identify several items that were completely up to code and not at all an issue. That inspector's write up intimidated the buyer in such a way that I had to make changes to satisfy the buyer and their agent, even though nothing was wrong in the first place. This included a breaker that had two small circuits hooked up as separate wires to the same breaker. The breaker was clearly labelled as being to code and approved for this double tapping usage, but the inspector flagged it anyway, presumably without squinting at the small text and diagram featured prominently on the breaker.

It is important that you do not allow yourself to lose enthusiasm for a transaction because of an overly negative slant on an inspection report. There are inspectors who absolutely could write a report that makes the newly completed penthouse in a luxury condo complex look like a massive code violation, fire hazard, and health and safety risk. Be aware that some inspectors believe they are being paid to do this. They are not telling you that the property is bad; their report is telling the seller that she is lucky to get rid of her unsafe, failure prone asset, and that it takes a lot of money to put all the components listed into *serviceable* state.

This is a negotiation tool creating fear in the seller that the property should be discounted a little more. When this ploy succeeds, a savvy buyer or buyer's agent will keep hiring that inspector, even though those reports may not accurately reflect the overwhelming soundness and quality of the structure you are looking to buy.

Once you have your inspection report in hand, you may request the seller to either make the repair(s) or issue a credit for the funds needed to make repairs. I have seen buyers get exceptional credits against the purchase price by assigning high price tags to items that they could fix for less money. However, on the flip side, you may find the seller, often coached by their agent, rejects most of the inspection claims and, basically, tells you to *take it or leave it.*

Especially in a strong seller's market, many sellers are selling the property mostly, or entirely, as is, and you either accept the defects found by the inspector, or the seller calls the other six people who submitted offers. This is common in the situation of a hot market like Colorado in the years 2014 through the time of writing in 2017, where there are numerous offers above list price for just about any property that is on the market.

I once benefited from a property falling out of contract due to inspection issues not being resolvable to both parties' satisfaction. I had been extremely frustrated after having offered significantly more than the list price and not having the seller accept my offer. However, two weeks later, I got a call asking if I still wanted the property. I jumped at moving forward with the purchase. The prior buyer had failed to reach agreement with the seller on inspection items and lost out on what, for me, has been a very good deal.

Closing

Closing is usually one of the easiest parts of your first real estate deal. It's an exciting part—a celebration day. You will have worked hard doing your numbers and analyzing the cash flows, getting insurance, working through all the paperwork that is associated with qualifying for a loan, doing an inspection, and so on.

A few tips to have a smooth closing:

- Make sure the numbers are correct. Title companies or closing attorneys occasionally have overworked closers who have a lot on their plate, and it's easy to make the wrong cut and paste.
- Make sure the tax prorations look right, and that the other various fees are in the right credit and debit columns.
- Work with your agent if you have any questions. Often, the 4 column credit and debits to both buyers and sellers settlement statements are quite complex and not entirely intuitive. The more complex the transaction is, with one or two or more loans, the more fees, credits, and prorations you will have. These include everything from loan junk fees to loan closing fees, to lender's title insurance, and so forth.

I had one real estate client who was a gifted mathematician, and he noticed the day of closing that the prorations were off $0.16. He convinced me he was right and the closer was wrong, yet asking for a reprinting of an entire new set of documents, before a 9 a.m. closing, on the busiest day of the month, was probably not worth the upheaval that $0.16 would have on any of the parties to the transaction.

Like anywhere in life, flexibility and a healthy dose of forgiveness are important. However, if the mistake is $16 or $160, it makes sense to be fully assertive and to insist on accuracy. I had one Dutch bank make an error of about $2,000 in their financial calculations and, unfortunately, that was in their favor. I was able to get them to correct most of it but, in the end, I still ended up short about $350, in what I wonder may have been a partially intentional math error. It's just when it's in the cents, and we're talking about a rounding error, I would not recommend over-emphasizing that level of accuracy. A mistake that's less than the cost of a side of avocado is probably not worth haggling about in the grand context of a real estate transaction. Even bigger mistakes are generally less than tuition at a good school.

Curing those Signature Cramps

One other comment: you may want to practice a simplified version of your signature. I used to walk out of closings, especially when there was a loan involved, and after 175 signatures, with a cramped arm. When I met Bob, and watched him scribble his *signature*, I had a major *aha* moment: Signing my *John Hancock* does not need to be difficult. I changed my signature, and I love it. Many comment on the simplicity and the elegance of how I sign with a flourish.

Sometimes my 12 year old son signs my credit card at restaurants when I ask him to. I've never had it go wrong, and I love my new signature. I now walk out of closings with a big smile rather than muscle cramps. If you are truly concerned about an easily imitable signature, feel free to embed a dot or other special little mark that most people trying to emulate your signature might not notice and, therefore, not copy.

Above all, after closing, go celebrate. The secret to living a happy life is to be aware of, and celebrate, all your wins. After closing, there's still more work to do, and this is the book that will teach you what to do to make that part of your rental career successful. Each time you have a win, like purchasing your first rental property, you deserve to celebrate. Well done!

Chapter 7

Making Your New Property Ready to Rent

"I am always doing that which I cannot do,
in order that I may learn how to do it."
Pablo Picasso

"I believe that people make their own luck
by great preparation and good strategy."
Jack Canfield

"There are no secrets to success. It is the result of preparation,
hard work, and learning from failure."
Colin Powell

"An ounce of prevention is worth a pound of cure."
Benjamin Franklin

If you're going to rent a place for a year, or maybe even two, make sure things are in the condition where you get to make repairs on your time, rather than having the tenant call you later with a problem, which of course at that point will be an emergency. This is kind of like doing proactive car repair rather than letting parts fail when they do, and ending up being stranded in the middle of the desert. Yes, you might be discarding components that are not entirely used up yet. Yet it is cheaper and less stressful, and a lot more peace of mind, to install a brand new dishwasher now than to have one fail the day before

Thanksgiving, when the tenant is getting ready for a big family Thanksgiving dinner and absolutely must have a dishwasher NOW.
It's not just about the maintenance and upkeep of the property. Tenants have rights, and one of them, in virtually all states other than Arkansas, is something called the warranty of habitability. In Colorado, for example, there are a number of rules regarding the minimum standards a rental property must meet. These include:

- Waterproofing and weather protection of roof and exterior walls maintained in good working order, including unbroken windows and doors;
- Plumbing or gas facilities that conformed to applicable law in effect at the time of installation and that are maintained in good working order;
- Running water and reasonable amounts of hot water at all times furnished to appropriate fixtures and connected to a sewage disposal system approved under applicable law;
- Functioning heating facilities that conformed to applicable law at the time of installation and that are maintained in good working order;
- Electrical lighting, with wiring and electrical equipment that conformed to applicable law at the time of installation, maintained in good working order;
- Common areas and areas under the control of the landlord that are kept reasonably clean, sanitary, and free from all accumulations of debris, filth, rubbish, and garbage and that have appropriate extermination in response to the infestation of rodents or vermin;
- Appropriate extermination in response to the infestation of rodents or vermin throughout a residential premises;
- An adequate number of appropriate exterior receptacles for garbage and rubbish, in good repair;
- Floors, stairways, and railings maintained in good repair;
- Locks on all exterior doors, and locks or security devices on windows designed to be opened that are maintained in good

working order; or

* Compliance with all applicable building, housing, and health codes which, if violated, would constitute a condition that is dangerous or hazardous to a Tenant's life, health, or safety, or otherwise unfit for human habitation

(Colorado Revised Statutes § 38-12-505)

What are some of the components most likely to fail?

I cover a comprehensive list of items below.

I would recommend replacing things that are in dubious condition before your tenant moves in. I talked to one property manager who said she likes to have the place repainted and re-carpeted before a tenant moves in, to avoid problems down the road. Sadly, she is off base. The carpet will not fail in the middle of the night and prevent a family from using the kitchen sink. However a clogged drain will, especially one that has been slow draining for a long time. In fact, that's what happened to her while she was on vacation in Europe. She called me to sort out a problem in her unit. Here's what happened. The kitchen drain had been clogged for a long time.

Clogged Drains and Drain Cleaners

When the tenant ran the kitchen drain, because the water had nowhere else to go, it would drain into the dishwasher. The tenant had tried unsuccessfully to use drain cleaning chemicals to clear the clog. What those chemicals (that claim they are safe for pipes when they are anything but) had done is actually eaten a hole in the pipe in the wall, and it had also damaged the dishwasher. Ultimately, there was a leak in the drain pipe in the wall; and because it was an older building, it was made out of cast iron pipe.

Drain cleaning chemicals are destructive to all pipes, but especially to cast iron drain pipes, and can cost you hundreds, if not thousands of dollars in repairs when they are used. The drain pipe leaking had caused wet carpet on the living room side of that wall, and the kitchen floor under the dishwasher was always wet as well. Ultimately, the drywall needed to be cut open, the deteriorated part of the drain cut out and replaced, and the dishwasher replaced as well. Then, the drywall needed to be repaired and repainted.

It's a good practice to add a clause to your lease, forbidding the use of these drain cleaning chemicals. Also, add another clause to your lease: if products that are not suitable for flushing, which include *supposedly* flushable wet wipes, tampons, and other feminine products, are pulled back by the roto rooter, you will charge them for that drain cleaning. However, I do think it's fair that if the issue stems from multiple generations of tenants rather than the current residents, you should be paying the bill if you have a tenant that you like and want to keep.

Roto Rooters

The only real way to address plumbing problems, especially in an older building with metal drain piping, is to call a plumbing professional, specifically called a Roto-Rooter. They use a long wire tool with cutting blades at the end, called a snake, to clear the drain. Fortunately, many cities have companies such as $99 Rooter or $89 rooter that will clean your drains without being inordinately expensive.

Common plumbing problems are hair and sanitary wipes in bath drains, and then just an overabundance of potatoes or carrots, or other food debris in kitchen drains. However, I have seen, on rare occasions, where tenants do crazy things: anything from flushing tampons to pouring hot candle wax down the drain. Both of these create clogs that require human intervention for the plumbing to be usable again. Even bacon grease or lard can become a serious problem over time, if poured down the drain rather than being disposed of by pouring it into a can and letting it cool before throwing it in the trash.

Hydro Jetting

My first property management company spent an entire month of my rent, $700, hydro jetting a drain where there was a grease clog preventing water from going through. With the grease, the Roto-Rooter snake would go through the clog and, then, after the snake was withdrawn, the grease would just sag back around the hole left by the snake tool and clog the drain again.

Hydro jetting is a comparatively expensive process where a tool that is essentially a power washer nozzle is inserted down the drain to try to flush any clogs into the city main.

Roofs

An important item to be proactive about is the roof. Inspect the roof occasionally, look for spots around chimneys or pipe penetrations where water might find its way to the interior of your property, and address with roof sealant. I prefer to address roofing issues before I see drywall damage in the ceiling, although I have heard other landlords recommend the opposite. My personal belief is that I want to only repair or replace the failing component, not a lot of ancillary components that are negatively impacted by the roof failure, which can include the ceiling drywall, light fixtures, interior walls, carpets or wood flooring, and mold.

If you do end up replacing a roof, my recommendation is that you go with the most expensive shingles or other material possible. It will gain you a noteworthy discount on your landlord's insurance. Most importantly, the extra durability more than offsets the increased cost of materials. The labor cost of installing shingles that may only last 10 years versus installing these shingles that could easily last 30 years, is identical. I am in this business for the long haul. It is important to be aware that not all *new roofs* are created equal.

Supply Hoses

Ultimately, there are not that many components that can fail in a costly manner, and most of them involve water. That includes your roof and silly things like poorly routed or disconnected gutters, and the extensions that direct water away from your basement. Another item that can have costly failures that again are easily avoidable are the washer supply hoses, which you should replace every time you get a new washer, dishwasher, or any other item that uses supply hoses—even faucets.

Stoves

Another note on buying appliances (many of my units have gas hookups for gas stoves): typically, gas stoves are very durable, and there are almost no moving parts to break. Buying a warranty on these is seldom necessary. However, with electric stoves, I have seen a recurring problem where the self-clean cycle creates so much heat that it fries electric components of the stove. My thought is that the cheaper stoves that lack the self-clean cycle can be a better bet for longevity.

Appliance Warranties

Items such as washing machines and dishwashers have a higher failure rate and can benefit from warranties. Some lower cost refrigerators often have poor quality compressors that are not really designed for extended use. A warranty will pay for the replacement if that happens to you. I remember I bought one refrigerator by a leading brand, and the compressor failed after a year and 2 months—essentially 60 days after the manufacturer's warranty expired. The catch 22 with warranties is that most of the times I buy a warranty, I don't need it, and the times I skip it, I end up needing it. It's almost like buying the warranty guarantees trouble free operation, while not buying it can result in needing to address the item later. I have not yet found an optimal balance.

Appliance Repair

I have found that appliance repair today is less viable than it was ten years ago. I used to routinely repair rather than replace appliances. Lately, the $75 or more trip charge to diagnose an appliance and tell me that a faulty part plus labor is virtually the same price to replace as the entire appliance, has made me just head directly to the scratch and dent section of my local home store/appliance store. It no longer seems worth applying much effort or expense to diagnose whether the appliance might even be worth saving.

Paint

Especially when you do a new paint job, seriously consider prohibiting smoking with strict penalties in the lease. Whether its marijuana or tobacco, I have found both leave a sticky, ugly residue that will bleed through new coats of paint, and even prevent the new coat of paint from adhering well.

To address this, you will need to pay extra to use some kind of acidic solution to clear that residue. This is something neither the person you are paying enjoys, nor that you will be happy to write a check for. It is important to remember that, generally, the security deposit will not cover the amount of damage that a tenant could conceivably create if they have no respect for your property, or worse, if they got mad at you. It is a good practice to always remain on good terms with your tenants and to create rules up front that prevent things that you are not in a good position to pay for later.

Furnaces

Furnaces often go bad, simply because elementary maintenance is not being performed. What I mean by that is that nobody is changing the filter. Clogged filters put so much more wear and tear on the unit. The motor must work harder to draw air through a filter that is clogged. Sometimes, if I haven't checked on a furnace in a year or two, the filter has turned into a solid piece of felt. In extreme cases, the furnace no longer has enough air flow moving through the heat exchanger to maintain the integrity of the metal, such that the heat exchanger cracks and allows the mixing of carbon monoxide with your indoor air, which creates a safety hazard and the urgent requirement to replace the entire furnace.

I have started advertising the benefits to the tenant of doing regular filter replacements. Periodically throughout the winter, I text all tenants with furnaces, reminding them that for the health of their lungs, changing the filters every 30 to 60 days is highly advisable. Filters are inexpensive, and I'm happy to supply them.

One thing I've noticed is that the more expensive, anti-allergenic filters are actually less good for the furnace. The better they claim to be at cleaning the air, the more restrictive they are in terms of not letting air flow through. I want the opposite. While we do need a filter to prevent particles from gumming up the blower wheel and the interior works as a furnace, we want a filter that is relatively free flowing so that the motor and other components do not have to work as hard.

Quality Units Beget Quality Tenants

Of course, it makes sense to install new carpet and new paint, which greatly increases the pride of having a nice home for the tenant. I often find there's a strong correlation between how nice the unit is when a resident moves in and how well they take care of it. It is hard for any resident to be proud of their home if it is clearly owned and managed by a slumlord. As I started doing more and more high-end, beautifully remodeled rentals, I noticed that I was really upgrading the quality of my tenants as compared to the bank owned units I had remodeled on a tight budget, where I just accepted the best tenants I could get.

Sometimes there seems to be a strong correlation between income level and general life skills, basic cleanliness, good common sense, and being financially astute in terms of being able to understand deadlines and the need to pay on time. I am finding that the more affluent applicants can make better tenants as a consequence.

Carpet

There are different schools of thought around carpet. On occasion, I have invested in really nice carpet, and then due to a bad tenant selection decision, have had that carpet completely ruined within six months. Other times, I have bought an extremely cheap carpet and have had it last five, six, or seven years, well past what that style of carpet should have lasted, but looking a little cheap and shabby for that extended duration. I wish I had bought the right carpet for the right tenant. There is always some element of *Murphy's Law* that we have to be prepared for.

Although it is increasingly rare to find one hundred percent nylon carpet, it is absolutely the best carpet, whether it's for a rental or for your own home. I own a property that for more than 10 years has had nylon carpet, and it's amazing. The standard polyester carpet that is now sold at most stores mats down when you walk on it a lot, even to the point that the fibers appear to somehow melt together, such that the original resilience and elevation of the fibers is not restorable. Nylon, on the other hand, does not have that limitation; it shows wear substantially less. Furthermore, nylon is much more stain resistant. It is amazing how clean a nylon carpet looks after a good carpet cleaning. Even in several cases where I thought the carpet might be ready for the trash, a good carpet cleaner was able to bring it all the way back. Unfortunately, many stores no longer carry carpet made out of nylon, and the cost benefits of purchasing nylon carpet if it is a low-volume, high price item, may not be justified. One final note on carpets:

Ensure You Get What You Paid For

"Trust, but verify."
Ronald Reagan

After some trial and error, I started purchasing my own carpet from the major home supply stores, having tradespeople install it, rather than paying for carpet and having others take control of delivering a product that I can't verify is the exact product I paid for. My experience has reinforced this as a best practice, and I know multiple other people who have had the same problem. Here's the scenario that created that realization: I pick out a nice beige carpet in the store. This may be several dollars more per square yard than what I intended to pay, but I was sold into it on the basis of quality, longevity, and the like.

I pay for the carpet and, a few days later, the repairman installs a beige carpet in my home. Months later, I realized that this is not the carpet I purchased—same color and general appearance, but an inferior grade. Somebody pocketed my money, substituted inferior carpet, and profited on the spread between what I paid and what they paid.

When I buy carpet and personally transport it to the job site, there is less opportunity for a bait-and-switch. This can also apply to the carpet padding. A friend of mine purchased *carpet, pad, and install* from a major home supply store. Specifically, she bought the most expensive, thickest, plushest, most water resistant pad offered. Nine months later, after a minor flood in her basement apartment, she peeled back the carpet only to notice that the pad that had been actually installed by the installer was a cheap version, rather than the exclusive, ultra-thick basement grade, water resistant, film backed, mold resistant carpet pad she had paid for. I got this account from her while she was in about hour five of continuing to try to resolve the issue with the national retailer, whose default reaction was to deny everything and claim their records are purged after 6 months. Every difficult experience has a lesson in it; in this case, it's to double check things and get the exact product I paid for, installed.

Paint

There is a strong case to be made for buying the best grade of paint that you can buy at a reasonable price. The new trend is that most of the home stores now have *Ultra Extra Special way beyond premium paints,* and I believe that those are essentially a slightly thicker version of the regular paint, priced at a significantly higher price. I buy the standard grade paint which, at the home retailer I shop at the most, is still termed *Premium,* and I get very satisfactory results. The few times I experimented with the more expensive paint, I could not notice a difference that would justify the cost differential.

I try to use consistent colors on all my units so that touch up is easy with just one color of paint in addition to the standard white I use for trim and doors. Once again, I like to supply the paint and keep the remainders. It is so easy for a chair to scrape against the wall; if you do not have a way of getting the right color, you most likely will have to repaint the whole wall, or even the whole room.

Many people say that professional paint stores have the best paint. I believe that is likely correct. At the same time, professional paint stores have limited opening hours, while I like to do my shopping when traffic is less, which includes nights and weekends. If the professional paint stores aren't open when I shop for paint, it makes no sense to rely on a brand and color of paint that it is challenging to gain access to.

The alternative around purchasing your own paint is to do what happened to my dad. He was moving into a new condo, found somebody he thought was trustworthy, and gave him the money to purchase paint. This guy painted my dad's entire condo one color—white—and then took the paint away with him, so that my dad couldn't tell what paint they had used. From inspecting the condo, I got the impression the painter just used Drywall Primer, which is the very cheapest way to make an area look white. However, primer is not a finish coat; it stains and shows blemishes, such as fingerprints, easily. In the end, I lined up a reliable painter who did the actual finish coats for my father, with paint I purchased and hauled up the elevator. Unfortunately, my dad ended up paying twice for a paint job, and also having twice the inconvenience.

Trusting people on the basis of them presenting a receipt is not a reliable way of verifying that the item on the receipt is what was installed or painted. It is so easy for an unsavory contractor to buy something, take it right to the returns desk for a refund, and then buy the cheaper version that he actually installs or paints on.

Verify Your Permits

> *"Trusting our intuition often saves us from disaster."*
> Anne Wilson Schaef

In that same vein, here is another note on dealing with contractors and permits: a couple years ago, I hired a sewer contractor to replace a sewer line on a single-family residence. I made sure that he promised to procure a permit on the job. When he was done, he camera-ed the line and showed me the video, which looked good. He also showed me the permit, which was signed and looked entirely official.

Unfortunately, I did not ask to keep a copy of that permit, nor did I verify it with the city. Later, when I called the city to check on the permit history for this property, there was no record of a sewer permit ever having been pulled or signed off on. It could be that this enterprising sewer contractor either used a blank sewer permit form available at the permits desk at the city, or he doctored one up using software and his laser printer. He then faked official signatures, and I had no clue that this official looking document would not be real.

I never imagined this contractor might have watched *Catch Me if You Can,* and actually applied what he saw, in his business. If I had been thorough, with a 10-minute or less phone call to the city permits desk, I would have found him out.

Paying Promptly to Get Prompt Attention Next Time

I personally really believe strongly in paying my trades people immediately when the job is done. It feels fair because I used to be a landscaper who didn't always get paid for the work I did. I know the contractors I treat fairly will want to come back and work for me again because of how I treat and pay them. At the same time, when things like fake permits go on, it doesn't make sense to pay at completion. Wait to verify the permit before releasing payment; relay my story if you need to justify why you can't just cut a check then and there. Once your payment is released, and especially once the check has been cashed, good luck getting any recourse.

Suing Contractors – It's Very Difficult to Collect

I once sued a different sewer contractor who also breached his contract and replaced only a portion of the sewer line rather than the entire line, which had been our agreement. I won in court. However, I was never successful in collecting the money I won. All his assets were titled in his wife's name; he had no bank accounts to garnish, and cashed all his checks at check cashing places.

After the fact, when it was too late, I realized this sewer contractor had several BBB ratings that reflected the same experience I had with him. He offered good prices, and people were either willing to overlook the BBB ratings, or they did what I did, which is to not take the time to check in the first place. It's another lesson to me. If something looks good, and it's a big ticket purchase, it's worth checking if it's too good to be true. I will save a lot of hassle by spending that extra 10 minutes on checking that everything is what it ought to be.

The sewage line industry seems to be exceptionally crappy (pardon the pun) in terms of the moral character of the contractors. I have gotten bids for $10,000 plus, for the same line I was able to get replaced for $1,900. Then, within that spectrum, the execution of the work has varied to being perfectly sound to being inadequate, such that a buyer cameraing the line once forced me to dig up sections to replace inadequate rubber fittings with the proper, steel banded, code approved fittings.

Finding Good Trades People

Where do you find good trade people? I must say I feel tremendously fortunate. I have a stable of great contractors. In 2008, when I was really expanding the size of my rental portfolio significantly, I didn't know anybody. A few times, I had called the Big Yellow Pages firms, and always felt like I was being ripped off when looking at the size of the bill versus the smallness of the repair, although I'm told advertising in a big way costs a fortune.

Todd, my plumber since 2008, says he used to work for a firm like that. The boss's requirement of their employees was that each service call should cost an average of $1,000. He tells of one night when he went to fix a water heater issue for a little old lady on fixed income. All that was wrong with the water heater was the $25 thermocouple that keeps the gas valve on when the pilot light is on. When Todd called the office, they said to charge her $1,000 for the repair, or try to upsell her to $3,000 for a new water heater. He felt this was a rip off, and ended up doing the repair for free, parking the work truck in their yard with the keys locked in it, and telling them to "go ____ themselves," and that he quits. He started his own business and has been a truly amazing advisor, friend, and incredibly experienced plumber, who always knows what to do. I found him on Craigslist.

Other trades people, I have found through recommendations, luck, and random coincidences that defy explanation. Malcolm Gladwell talks of people who are connectors. I work with an electrician, Alan, who is such an individual. He knows all kinds of people who have been greatly helpful to me, including a drywaller, a tiler, a cement guy, a good mechanic, and a few more.

Perspective: Most of the Time, All Goes Well

"Always in life, bad times will lead to great times."
M. Night Shyamalan

"Everything is ok in the end. If it's not ok, it's not the end."
Unknown

I want you to know that these experiences I am relaying are on the extreme end of the spectrum of dealing with contractors and tenants. Yet it's better you read my stories and address the risks they present up front, rather than adding your own learning experiences to the mix, especially if your story is just a similar version of one of mine. For every risk, there are multiple ways you can mitigate them. By exposing you to these risks, I am educating and empowering you to deal with them. Furthermore, a story where everything just went according to plan, as it mostly does, is not that exciting of a story.

The key element is that there is some trial and error here, and that if we are afraid to make mistakes, we won't learn, and we won't achieve the things we can accomplish when we embark on projects.

Some projects seem like nothing goes right but, in the end, we come out OK financially, and we are a lifetime wiser for everything that goes wrong. This can seem horrible at the time but is a huge win at the end. How else would we really learn?

Chapter 8

Property Management

"Property management is sometimes like Algebra.
You look at X and wonder Y."
Unknown

"Hard work beats talent when talent doesn't work hard."
Unknown

"The best way to predict the future is to invent it."
Alan Kay

"Effective management always means asking the right question."
Robert Heller

Managing Your Property Management Firm

Property management firms fill a vital role in the marketplace. There's an area of critical mass where no owner can keep track of 5,000 apartments, or 500, or maybe even 50. Yet, there is risk in placing too much trust in property managers and property management firms. I worked with four property management firms, and I found all wanting over time.

The first I hired seemed quite good in the early stages, but then I noticed that vacancies took forever to fill, sometimes as long as 3 to 6 months. I was remodeling a triplex and had already completed the first unit, which was being advertised as being for rent. I was working on the adjacent unit, and people would come up, saying that they had scheduled a showing with the property management firm, but the representative from the property management firm never showed, and stood them up.

When calling the property management firm to ask about this, they denied these assertions. After a couple recurrences of the same story, I ended up figuring out it was the owner's son who had been delegated to perform these showings. Near the property was a street known for having drug dealers and the like. My theory is that driving by that area, the son could not resist the lure of illegal temptations, and consequently did not make it to the showing.

Since I was there enough, I ended up being able to show the property to tenants and get it rented. Since I was doing their property management work for them, I ended up parting ways with this firm. One of the fundamental challenges for property management firms is that the rewards for providing the level of service they're expected to provide are inadequate. For example, I personally would not choose to become a property manager. Receiving a trivial 8 or 10% of rents for being available 24/7, with both tenants and owners expecting me to jump on a dime and cancel all plans to respond to an *emergency* that may or may not truly be urgent, is not the way I wish to live my life. After the initial bad experience with missed showings and long vacancy times with the first property management firm, I hired a real estate agent who was a colleague and friend of Gina's, my amazing real estate broker, as my property manager.

The first property management firm transferred $14,000 of my security deposits to him; this person, whom I won't name, enthusiastically took on managing my properties. In the beginning, he was an amazing manager. He was cheerful, enthusiastic, on the ball, and creative about fixing things. He wished to help me and learn from me, and to support me in my remodels. It just felt like a great win-win. Unfortunately, that euphoria did not last.

One of the aspects of property management is record keeping and accounting that is mundane, boring, and time-intensive. This was especially true for some of my small, multi-family properties that were master metered, so there was one meter serving several tenants. We had created ratio utility billing systems (RUBS) formulas, apportioning a certain percentage of the utilities to each unit, based on the number of occupants and the size of the unit.

Staying on top of monthly billings took a good amount of spreadsheet jockeying, and it appears my property manager fell behind. I was engaged buying new units and remodeling them, and working a full-time job. I expected him do his job, as I was doing multiple jobs of mine. Unfortunately, he wasn't, and I wasn't paying attention to notice.

The monthly reports I got were thick stacks of QuickBooks reports that were often 110 pages or more. What I realize now is that they were often accrual basis reports, essentially stating the money that *should have* come in per the contracts. What I should have been getting were cash basis reports stating the money that *actually* came in. This was an expensive way of learning how accounting works. Yet I learned it much better than by being in a boring MBA finance class, slugging Mountain Dew, while trying not to fall asleep in a very uncomfortable chair/desk combo.

Soon, it became apparent that my property manager had been using the security deposit funds to pay the utility bills without invoicing the tenants in a timely manner, and without putting much effort into collecting shortfalls when tenants weren't paying rents or utilities.

Utility bills in the winter cold season can easily be $150 a month. Neglecting to invoice these for three or four months creates a sizable past due obligation to the tenant. In a number of cases, the size of that past due billing was such that low-income tenants were no longer in a position to pay in one payment. Tenants were falling behind, and I was stuck with unpaid utility bills, while needing to pay the power and gas company to keep the lights and heaters on, regardless of the fact that these expenses were not being reimbursed.

An accounting audit I took on when the problem became evident, unveiled that there was approximately $5,000 in utilities that I would not be able to collect. When firing this property manager, I was unable to get the $14,000 security deposits returned to me. He created what I can only consider fake invoices, charging me for work he never did, and the $14,000 in security deposits that are neither his or my money, but money that belongs to the tenants, had vanished like water poured on sand.

I reported this agent to the Colorado Real Estate Commission; they investigated over several months and then fined him. There is a questionable ethicality to a government agency fining a thief. Since the government has much more enforcement power than me, the person who was stolen from, the government agency is telling the thief to give them funds that were stolen from me. This makes it much more difficult for the thief to repay me the monies stolen from me.

The Real Estate Commission told me the only way I could get my money back is through suing this property manager. He had a drug-addicted daughter in New Orleans, as well as several other younger children and other family obligations, so he simply did not have the money to easily repay me. He did cough up the money owed to the state commission but, predictably, that left him even more in a position where he would not be able to reimburse me. In the end, I chose to let it go. In reviewing other cases, my case was not that extreme. I came across one case where a property manager took approximately $100,000 in security deposits, flew to Las Vegas, and lost or otherwise spent the entire sum of money.

Later, I hired another property management firm because I was still working full-time, and I could not handle the volume of calls during business hours when I had an apartment that was listed for rent. This firm again was very good for the first three or four months of the engagement. Then, they may have decided that for the amount of work that they had taken on, the compensation contractually negotiated was not adequate.

To remedy this, they devised strategies to increase their income. This included padding repair bills or just seemingly making them up. It included collecting late fees from tenants for late payments but not remitting them to me as the owner, even though the property management agreement did not allow them to retain the $100 late fees that are in my standard lease.

They also appear to have entered into bill padding agreements with the service providers they recommended we use, that they had relationships with. For example, if a furnace repair bill actually might have cost in the $200 ballpark, I got the impression that they would have the repair person write the invoice for $300, and pocket the difference. I think I was fortunate in being suspicious about property management firms, and ferreting out some of this inappropriate behavior early before it cost me too much money.

I credit the story relayed to me by another real estate investor. He was dating the owner of the property management firm and, as they were about to go for a drive in his convertible, he heard her yell to her assessment assistant, "Hey, Barbie, what was the net income on the McDonald property this month?" Barbie yelled back, "Six hundred dollars." The owner of the firm replied to Barbie, "Bill them $500 for repairs," before leaving out the door to go for the drive with her date. My property management relationships all started off well, but the pattern of declining service and increasing costs emerged in the five firms I've interacted with. Consequently, since no longer working in a full time day job, I have been self-managing. What I have noticed is that property management is not even close to the amount of work that the property managers always used to complain to me that it was. I guess that was just how they were justifying the high fees they were charging.

Property Management Best Practices

Next, I know that I cannot scale like this forever; at some point, as I acquire more properties, or larger properties, I will need to go back into trusting and managing a person or organization to handle things for me. However, there are best practices I can recommend for property management:

- Do not allow the property management firm to hold security deposits. Keep the deposits in your bank account where they cannot go missing without your involvement.
- Do not allow the property management firm to collect rents. Have rents be mailed to you or deposited to your accounts. Do allow the property management firm to have ready access to who paid and who didn't, so that they are still in the position of handling the drudgery of bookkeeping.

One way I would do this is by having two accounts with online access visible to the property management firm. One account I share with tenants who like to do direct deposits, or walk in deposits at the bank. As soon as payments clear, I transfer all funds to the other main account, whose account information I don't share with tenants. This is where I deposit all mailed checks, and the main account that I run all mortgage payments and vendor payments out of. I access the account daily while rents are due, and update the deposit description in online banking to show the name and address of the tenant that each payment came from for ease of verifying who paid.

- Contract with repair providers directly, instead of allowing the property management firm to do so. If you have the relationship, and are the point of contact for repairs, it is less likely that there are fluffed up invoice charges that are being pocketed by the property manager, rather than the true costs just being passed on to you.
- Drive by properties frequently and document the maintenance issues you take care of. I had a co-worker with a rental property out of state, in Louisiana near where his dad lived. His dad had gone over to the property; he had brought a ladder and cleaned the gutters. Two weeks after his dad's visit to the property, my co-worker was invoiced $75 from the property management firm for cleaning gutters.

Check out the firm's licensing status. In Colorado, property managers are required to be licensed real estate agents. Similar rules exist in most other states, although states like Kansas, Idaho, Maine, Maryland, Massachusetts, and Vermont don't require property managers to be licensed. It does seem reasonable that most of the unsavory property management activities are carried out by unlicensed persons, who would be harder to have any enforcement over.

Even in Colorado, where licenses are required for the manager of a property management firm, many firms hire unlicensed persons for work, whether or not the state rules actually sanction this or not.
A red flag worth noting is if the licensing agent is playing fast and loose with the rules, which could indicate that they would play fast and loose with your money as well. I've had an instance of this. One property management firm I engaged was licensed in the name of a broker who was full-time at the fire department, and never, to my knowledge, did any property management activities. All the actual work was done by his unlicensed cousin and various other family members. That ignoring of the rules alone should have been a red flag.

The unlicensed cousin quickly graduated into collecting money, like $100 late fees from tenants, and not reporting or remitting the money to me as property owner—in a word, theft. In this case, a business partner of mine filed a Real Estate Commission complaint against the firm. Interestingly, regarding enforcement when checking their license status, there was no record of disciplinary actions on file.

Do Property Management Yourself before Outsourcing It

A key recommendation is for you to do property management yourself for at least a while. Do not buy a property and turn it over immediately to a property manager. Once you have done the job yourself, you will understand the amount of time required for certain aspects of the job, and you will have a much better idea when somebody is telling you things that aren't true. You will have figured out your own tricks of the trade, and you will ask better questions when you interview and evaluate property management firms. You will be so much better at looking at the expenses they incur, compared to what you spent. In short, you will know how to identify areas where things are not being done above board.

My analogy is that of the old corporate adage, which was to start in the mail room and then work your way up to CEO. If you just start by managing managers, you will not know the questions to ask, or the signals to look for, to be the very best manager of managers of your own property and prosperity that you can be. Furthermore, we all respect people who are successful in life, yet who don't hesitate to grab a broom or mop and help out with the details.

As in many areas in life, we are rewarded for stepping outside our comfort zone. We are rewarded for taking risks, for being courageous, for taking the initiative to learn new things, and for being willing to be a little busier than the average person who spends 35 hours a week watching TV.
(https://www.nytimes.com/2016/07/01/business/media/nielsen-survey-media-viewing.html)

Do take on being a property manager, even if you set a firm time limit like 3 months or 6 months of being a property manager on your own before delegating to the pros. You will likely find, after you have placed a good tenant, that you very rarely get calls, and that there is almost no work until the tenant moves out. This learning may prompt you into finding creative ways of partnering with a property management firm simply for the leasing portion of the property management component, and taking on the day-to-day property management yourself.

Many firms will be reluctant to do this because they know the 10% commission they collect each month is gravy, and the vast majority of the work is up front getting the tenant. You might get lucky and find somebody to help you with just the finding and screening portion of property management, but I still recommend finding your first one or two tenants yourself, or at least being heavily involved in the process, such as being present at open houses and showings. That way, you really understand the drill, and you get to have a full, in-depth understanding of an important part of your financial future.

Section 8 and Other Subsidized Housing Programs

Some landlords really like Section 8 programs for acquiring tenants. Section 8 is where a local Housing Organization pays some or all the rent for low-income tenants. There are advantages to this: one, the rent that is paid by the housing organization is deposited in your account, punctually, on the first of the month.

There's also a shadow side. I, personally, often tell tenants that I will not accept Section 8 vouchers anymore. Here's why: on one property, there was something missing from the paperwork that I had submitted to Section 8. And because of incomplete paperwork, the housing agency put a hold on rent payments to me, yet did not notify me so that I could correct the issue. I only learned of this when I got a call that the lease was going to be cancelled, and that I would not get any compensation for the time the tenant had stayed at my unit if I didn't address the missing paperwork in one business day. In the end, the agency took 3 months to give me my first rent check. For many landlords, this would not be a happy situation.

In another case, a Section 8 tenant moved from one of the housing projects owned by Section 8, into my unit. However, she had not returned her house key to the Section 8 office. Please be aware that a key costs around $2 to $3 to duplicate. It took this woman 6 days to return the keys to the housing office. The cost, assigned to me by the Housing Agency for her oversight, was the docking of 6 days rent. The logic may have been that by not having returned the key, the rent money should still be going to the Section 8 Project Housing rather than to me, her new landlord.

This tenant occupied my unit for free, for 20% of the month, because the housing office hadn't received a $2–$3 key back in time.

Also, there is a truism in life that things that people get for free aren't considered to be very valuable. This can even apply to a very valuable rental property. What's more, rent subsidized, unemployed residents, who spend almost 24-hours a day at home, put way more wear and tear on your kitchen, bathroom, furnace, carpets, and all the other elements of your property. Moreover, because such tenants are home all the time, issues like a clogged toilet are not something that can wait until they get home from work they don't have. Instead, any issue must be fixed right away.

Working tenants who are home for less time are much more appreciative of the housing because they actually pay for it, and create less wear and tear. Therefore, I prefer renting to them.

Furthermore, I like to do 18-month or 2 year leases, yet my local Section 8 office only allows a maximum of one year leases. So, I often end up in the scenario where a tenant who has put much more wear and tear on my property, moves out after one year, where I then lose the 13th month of rent to a rehab project while the unit is vacant. I would rather have had a more long-term tenant who may have treated the unit much better by not being around as much, all other things being equal.

One last point to notice is that, often, the Section 8 units have more occupants than stated on the lease. While this is frowned upon by the Section 8 agency, it is exceedingly common and something that is not to my advantage to report. I do not want to penalize the tenant such that they would move out of my unit on bad terms, which is not where a smart landlord wants to be in terms of getting their unit back in the best shape possible. Moreover, if I report them for things where the main Section 8 penalty is revoking the tenant's housing voucher, I am creating a premature vacancy in my unit by flagging non-compliance with the rules to the Section 8 office. This creates a Catch-22 that doesn't serve me or the tenant.

Most section 8 tenants have a monthly co-pay. At its lowest, it is $10, or some token monthly sum, or as high as the substantial portion of the rent, say 50% of the rent. The copay portion of the rent can be challenging to collect, especially with those tenants paying a lower amount like $30 or so, as the sum doesn't justify a ton of effort on invoicing and collections.

Moreover, there are some tenants who get the impression that I, the *wealthy landlord*, could just forgive that portion of their rent payment. Also, the Section 8 office can seemingly, at will, at any interval, change the tenants' co-pay, sometimes without my getting a notification. In some cases when I was less diligent about my bookkeeping, the tenant copay had gone up, while my invoices to the tenant still showed the old, lower amount. The tenant paid the lower amount instead of the DHA required amount (and without notifying me of my invoicing error). Later on, I would do an audit, and discover that I was short several hundred dollars. Sometimes I have been able to get this amount of money back; other times I have not.

Finally, if the tenant ever gets annoyed with the landlord, they have some powerful weapons to use against them. One of the housing organization's standard, mandatory lease terms is that if the heating system or the water system is out of commission for 24 hours, the lease is automatically terminated.

In one instance, my tenant made a complaint to the Housing Organization that the heating system was not working. They sent out an inspector and determined that, in fact, it was working, and the complaint was unjustified. However, at that time, I was out of the country, and the tenant also chose not to notify me. It could have easily happened that I would have not addressed the situation because of not being notified, or because of not being able to get an HVAC professional in the short time required, and that the government organization would have terminated the lease.

My perspective, flawed as it might be, is that working tenants are busy creating value for their families and their employers, while those who are home, unemployed and on welfare, have a lot of leisure time, which sometimes is spent on unwholesome things that don't serve me or society as a whole.

All Cash Move-Ins

Numerous times, I have been offered all cash for the first month's rent and the security deposit, in exchange for a move-in that same day. Often, the tenant is asking me to skip the screening process; clearly they have so much money that they must be a great tenant, right? They may tell other stories, such as that they are a landlord too, but their unit is rented and they need somewhere to live right now.

Consistently, I have stood my ground and stated clearly that "my boss doesn't allow me to skip the screening process." Invariably, the tenant screening report shows several assertions the tenant made to be nonfactual, causing me to wonder what else they said that isn't true.

I love that the screening reports provide a point of view that I can use to guide my intuition. Occasionally, my intuition tells me something negative, but the tenant is so great at telling stories that push all the right buttons that I am tempted to silence my intuition and buy into the wonderful stories the applicant is telling. The tenant's credit and criminal records tell a story.

I sometimes wonder if that one woman I really came close to renting to was planning on using my property as a meth lab. She looked OK and was even dressed in a business suit. Yet, when I insisted on meeting her boyfriend, he was skinnier than Gandhi, nervous and twitchy, and had the skin lesions that are consistent with heavy meth usage.

Tenants with Prior Evictions

I do not recommend leasing to people with prior evictions. Often, people with prior evictions beg and sweet-talk you to convince you that they're a great tenant, that the mistake in the past typically wasn't their fault at all, and now they're being penalized for it unfairly. They want you to overlook the fact that they have an eviction, and just allow them to rent your place.

My advice is, "No." The first time a tenant gets evicted, they are often blindsided; they are not familiar with the process, and their landlord is able to get them out for a violation such as non-payment, drug dealing, or other serious violations of the lease that justify a judge signing an eviction order.

However, after having been through the process once, some tenants learn how to misuse the system to make any subsequent evictions very challenging. It is best to simply avoid this problem by not accepting people with a prior eviction. While past performance is not a guarantee of future behavior if they've had problems before, they have a higher likelihood of allowing them to happen again. Also, their record already has a stain on it, so there is less incentive to maintain a clean record.

Tenant Screening

I look at my tenant screening as a way of measuring a tenant's *integrity score*. What does a screening report really tell you? Firstly, if they pay their bills; secondly, if they pay the rent and, in the case of some collections items and judgments reported against them, if they left a prior residence in such poor shape that the prior landlord pursued them for damages. By pulling their criminal record, I can also see if they have a problem with drugs, with driving drunk, with speeding tickets, with disturbing the peace, or other silly offenses that make me raise my eyebrows as I peruse the list.

I've had property managers who recommend a cheap, online credit screening tool offered by one of the major evictions bureaus, which they thought was adequate and sufficient screening. I strongly disagree. Just because it costs a third of what I pay, does not make it a good screening. Getting the wrong tenant does not create a difference between $30 and $13; the impact is going to be significantly larger.

I, therefore, insist that I always check all three items: credit, criminal, and evictions.

Credit reflects integrity. When I get a tenant applicant in July, who in March went into collections status with T-Mobile for promising to pay a monthly fee for his handset and the monthly services, and then failed to fulfill that agreement, that tells me this tenant has a problem with keeping his commitments, especially where they involve paying on time for the benefits he receives.

The same applies when they owe money to the power company, the cable company, the company that issued the gas station credit card, or the company that issued a clothing credit card or department store credit card. If they do not keep agreements with all these merchants, why would they make an exception for me? If one or more parties the tenant has done business with is making a written record that this person is not trustworthy, I put a lot of stock in that. The occasions in my early career as landlord, when I paid more attention to the tenant's promises than the documented blemishes in the credit report, I came to regret my naiveté and kindness toward a person who didn't deserve them.

I make an exception in one instance, and that is medical collections. I see this too often: a good person has an accident or gets sick. They go to the doctor or hospital. Next thing they know, they owe thousands of dollars. Medical bills can quickly become crippling. In one survey, "researchers found that the treatment price for a headache could range from $15 to a whopping $17,797. As for a sprained ankle, it could set someone back a paltry $4, or up to $24,110!" (*http://www.foxbusiness.com/features/2013/06/27/outrageous-er-hospital-charges-what-to-do.html*)

After 90 days of nonpayment and non-negotiation with the provider, those bills go on this person's credit report. Based on a choice I make, if all other things are indicating good character on the part of the tenant, I will heavily discount the weight assigned to medical collections on their credit report.

Bankruptcy

Bankruptcy is the nemesis of landlords. I got caught up in this once. A tenant filed bankruptcy specifically to avoid eviction. What happens is the bankruptcy judge will automatically *stay* an eviction, which means that they will put a hold on any eviction proceedings.

The logic is that the tenant has valuable assets that other creditors can seize to mitigate their losses in bankruptcy. I, the landlord, got to be the free storage facility for those assets. This is a scary prospect. This particular tenant got 6 months' rent free, and I had to hire a bankruptcy attorney to overturn the stay of eviction, then returning to County Court to reinitiate a new eviction because the old one expired. My total legal fees in this one eviction were north of $7,000. The legal firm I hire to do evictions found this to be an unusual case they hadn't seen before. At the eviction I finally won, six months later, they had three of their attorneys present, along with my separate bankruptcy attorney, to prevent any further travesties of justice.

Bankruptcy rules provide certain conditions after an initial bankruptcy as to when a new bankruptcy can be filed. That means that somebody who recently filed bankruptcy cannot as easily refile and, as a landlord, your risk is limited. However, the longer it's been since someone filed a previous bankruptcy, the more likely it is they could file a new one. Watch the items on their credit to see if there would be motivation for considering a new bankruptcy filing. This particular problem tenant had filed for a prior bankruptcy 7 years ago. On the morning the sheriff met me at 10 a.m. at the property to fulfill the eviction, dump this tenants possessions on the curb and change the locks, that tenant came running up with a piece of paper from the US Bankruptcy Court, with a stay of eviction he had succeeded in getting that morning. The sheriff told me to change the lock back, and left once I had done that.

That is when my $7,000 in legal fees and 6 months of free rent began, along with enormous electricity bills while the tenant was growing marijuana inside my property, rent free, with no possibility of me enforcing the terms of the lease, courtesy of the US Bankruptcy Court. Note, this tenant was inherited from the previous owner of the six-plex I had bought as my second rental property ever. If I had screened this tenant, there would have been lots of red flags to not accept him as a tenant. As it was, I got the property at a discount and sold it 13 months later for a large profit that made up for my heartburn and costs.

Performing Evictions

When performing an eviction, always hire a lawyer. Here's why:

On my first eviction, I tried to evict a tenant myself. I went to the court and got educated by the staff there. I collected the required forms, and filled out all the right forms correctly. I showed up at court on the appointed day, as did the tenant. The judge said, "Oh, you are filing for an eviction on behalf of an LLC; do you have a letter of permission from the LLC authorizing you to pursue this eviction?" I was completely taken aback, and stammered, "No." The judge dismissed the case and told me to work things out with the tenant who had promised the judge that he would make payments.

After the dismissal, this individual never made good on those promises. I stayed in the courtroom for a few minutes, disappointed, confused, and very frustrated. I am an MBA grad; I took my required course work in business law, and prima facie grounds for evictions were being completely ignored by a judge on a minor technicality. I couldn't believe it! I watched the attorney from the leading evictions firm hammer through a stack of evictions in less time than my single, unsuccessful eviction had taken.

The lawyer presented a piece of paper and said a few words to the judge, who stamped the order for eviction; the lawyer handed over the next piece of paper to the judge, and got the same outcome of a rubber stamp approval, and so on.

I had met this attorney in the elevator on the way up to court, and he had given me his card. When I needed to re-evict this tenant, and for the six or seven tenants I've had to evict since, I used this lawyer and his firm. The entire service cost approximately $350. I no longer needed to show up in court. The job got done. There are certain things that are just meant to be outsourced, and this is clearly one of them for me.

Alternatives to Eviction

When considering eviction, be aware of a crucial fact. You can spend money on the lawyer—in my case, about $350. Then, there's a waiting period. There's a wait between the filing and the court hearing. Once you get the judge's order for eviction, there's a wait for the sheriff to have availability to perform the physical eviction, which can be somewhere between 10 days to 3 weeks, in Denver County. Then, I need to show up with at least four laborers who are able to carry the entire contents of the apartment to the curb in the space of approximately an hour. If I do not have enough help, the sheriff is likely to cancel the eviction. That sheriff service costs another $125.

Or I could make a deal with a non-paying tenant, and say, "I will give you cash for keys." I tell the tenant to leave the unit in broom swept condition and, upon surrender of the keys, say next Saturday at 7 p.m., I will give them a check for $350. I can save a little bit of money compared to the approximately $500 for a complete eviction, and definitely save myself time.

Moreover, I am likely to save on damages that the tenant could do prior to an inevitable eviction, since I am paying them and inspecting the unit prior to writing them a check, rather than parting on extremely bad terms.

I know it feels wrong. Rewarding somebody financially because of bad behavior is horrible. This is the equivalent of negotiating with terrorists. Yet going to war using the legal and law enforcement route will cost me more in time and money, and possibly frayed nerves.

I have learned to be pragmatic and outcome focused. Do I give them less money than I would pay otherwise to get them on their way and be about mine? Yes! One thing I've learned in this business, and in life in general, is that people who collect small sums of money for being a bad person, like that tenant, will remain a poor loser most of their life.

If I make smart, goal oriented decisions, even when that means doing something that just seems temporarily unfair to me, I win in the end. In the end, I still own the property, and I will make my money back, and then some. Therefore, I've decided to even treat bad people well. I'll give them a couple hundred bucks, and move on. My life is better for it and, if I get to make their life better too, that does not take anything away from my good karma.

Collections

For taking the burden of suing the tenant off my hands, and actually tracking them down and trying to collect, a typical collections agency will take 40 to 50% of the money they collect as their commission. This is a highly specialized discipline and, for me, it's one of those things I am best off outsourcing. The whole collections arena has a lot of complexity and regulation that is well outside of my purview.

I have used the same collections agency since I started being a landlord. It is an agency that specializes in collecting from tenants for landlords. I would say, in my case, approximately half of the money that I have referred for collections does get collected. That means, after the agency's cut, I'm getting roughly a quarter of the money owed. There were some cases where tenants, for a long time, didn't seem to care about paying; then, all of a sudden, they must have gotten serious about their life, and maybe thought about buying a house or otherwise cleaning up their credit. These former tenants did start paying off balances that were two, three, or four years old, often negotiating a lump sum payment, lower than the actual balance and interest accrued that they owed.

I do find it is worth the effort to go ahead with trying to collect, even from tenants I am doubtful to ever be able to get money back from. Even if the collections agency is not able to recover money, they are able to put negative items on the tenant's credit, as well as having any judgements show up against the tenant. These serve as a warning to my fellow landlords who might be considering them as a tenant. One of the services we can do for each other as landlords, is to not allow abusers of the process to become serial abusers of the process, who do what they did to us, to others.

When using a collections firm, the preparatory part of collections is relatively simple. At its core, it's about compiling the documentation that is adequate for the collections firm to file suit against a tenant and win a judgment. This means that we need to be thorough in our record-keeping. I need to have the tenant sign a disclosure that everything is in good condition at the time of moving in, except for any items that are listed by the tenant. I need pictorial records of before and after, such as a picture of the pre-move-in bathtub, and the after-move-out bathtub, with any chips or other damage the tenant created. Likewise, pictures or video of pre- move-in walls and doors, and after-move-out documentation of any blemishes or holes a careless tenant may have created.

Next, I need to retain the application form, which includes data details like Social Security numbers that help collections agencies do a skip trace on the tenant, and then report derogative items on their credit report.

Tenant Applications

Especially if you use a property management firm with an online application process, make sure at the time of application that you actually get the tenants social security number. I just had this come up recently.

A tenant was procured a long time ago by a property management firm that a partner and I engaged. The tenant ended up not paying rent anymore. This particular property management firm was very proud of their process that this tenant went through. The property management firm had the tenant go to a national credit reporting firms website, hot linked from the property managements firm's site, and enter and all their data. A report got emailed to the property management firm, which they used to accept the applicant.

However, to comply with all the federal rules about data security, the social security number and other details that the tenant entered for the screening report to be generated were not made available to the property manager by the national screening firm.

Now, since this property management firm and I parted on bad terms, I wouldn't be able to get that information, even if by chance they did have it. This means that pursuing collections against the tenant if they leave owing a balance was probably never available to the property manager, and is definitely not available to me.

Leases

Each state has specific variations around landlord tenant laws and, therefore, I cannot provide a sample formulaic lease in this book. In my state, Colorado, there's a local publishing company called Bradford Publishing that publishes a lot of different legal forms, which include a good sample lease. For my own lease, I used excerpts from that, as well as good clauses from leases where I used to rent, and I continue augmenting my lease over time as things occur that I want to prevent. Examples of clauses I added are:

- keeping the furnace on during winter months, even when leaving on vacation
- not allowing smoking inside units
- the tenant initials that the units are bed bug free at the time of

tenant move-in, and that any bed bug issues that occur afterwards are fully and solely the responsibility of the tenant to address
- if I need to replace a lock for any reason, I charge $50, plus the cost of the lock. This addresses the ex-boy/girlfriend issue where, after a breakup, the other party had the key, and the tenant on the lease wants to change the locks. I got tired of doing this for free because my lease didn't have a provision for it.

Your state may have a similar publisher specializing in legal forms, or you may be able to attend a local REIA (Real Estate Investor's Association) and get some good leads on a lease for you to use or modify.

In the end, my conviction is that good tenants don't require a lot of referring to the lease. The main elements are the length of the lease, the rent amount and, when the rent is late, how much the late fee is. The remaining items I have rarely had any real discussion on. I don't want to minimize the importance of having a good lease with respect to all the other clauses, yet I want to emphasize that it is not terribly challenging to find a lease you can start with, which you can improve over time.

Calling Landlords for References

Landlord references are always invaluable. Most landlords understand the value of sharing our experiences so that one person's bad experience does not become another person's bad experience. We see companies like Uber and Airbnb who have institutionalized this process. Everybody, both landlord and tenant, has references that potential business associates can see, and where any party that does not do business in an ethical manner gets screened out of the community. Unfortunately, in the much bigger landlord-tenant business, there is no good system for that yet.

A big thing to note is whether the landlord you are calling for a reference still has the tenant living with them or not. There is the potential that a landlord, who has a terrible tenant that is still living with them, could give false information that helps the tenant get out of their hair, and into yours. However, if the tenant has left, and there is no impact to the landlord regardless of what they say, you are much more likely to get the truth.

I get annoyed at the big property management firms who, as a matter of policy, will not give references on the first call. Often, they will say things like, "I need to fax a release," or "I need the tenant's permission for the firm to release information." My application has a clause that tenants are agreeing for the release of reference information to me. Yet I am reluctant to submit the signed application to just anyone, with all the other confidential tenant information. Even if I jump through all the hoops with the paperwork larger property management firms require to provide a reference, a typical large property management firm will often still provide virtually worthless information. This is something along the lines of "yes, they mostly paid on time," or, "we can't find any record of complaints." The big property management firms, like us, are in a business where we make valuable assets available to people for a small monthly fee. It would be nice if there was a spirit of corporate responsibility to openly share data that helps us all protect our assets.

Yes, some of that unwillingness to tell the truth is due to the litigious legal climate that we live in today, yet it is annoying when a property management firm calls me for a tenant reference, and I give them the details they need to know; yet if I call the same firm back 15 days later about a tenant leaving their complex wanting to move into one of my units, they will not reciprocate with the same transparency.

Our job is to make do with what we can get and, sometimes, between the lines of the safe, content free statements made by the institutional property management firms, there are data points we can get value from. For example, I like to ask: "Did you personally, or someone in your office, have to deal with this individual in terms of collecting late rents, or addressing noise or pet complaints?" Occasionally, by making it about the individual I am speaking to, I can honor them. Sometimes they reciprocate by sharing details that a more impersonal interaction with them would not have elicited.

Chapter 9

The Mindset of Successful Landlords

*"Once your mindset changes, everything on the
outside will change along with it."*
Steve Maraboli

*"There are no limitations to the mind except those we acknowledge.
Both poverty and riches are the offspring of thought."*
Napoleon Hill, *Think and Grow Rich*

*"The goal is not to simply eliminate the bad, which does
nothing more than leave you with a vacuum, but to pursue
and experience the best in the world."*
Timothy Ferriss, *The 4-Hour Workweek*

*"If you don't sacrifice for what you want,
what you want becomes the sacrifice."*
Unknown

*"If you are insecure, guess what? The rest of the world is, too.
Do not overestimate the competition and underestimate
yourself. You are better than you think."*
Timothy Ferriss, *The 4-Hour Workweek*

What to Say if Asked, "Are You the Owner?"

I try not to let people know I am the owner, although many tenants
are smart and figure it out eventually. My favorite answer to "are you

the owner?" is "I wish." That answer is true, most of the time. The bank still owns a chunk of most of my properties, and I would gladly own the property free and clear.

Especially at move-in, there is no benefit to thumping my chest and telling people I am the owner. It is easier to say *no* to requests when I am just the manager who lacks authority to say *yes* to non-standard requests. I can be the person on the tenant's side dealing with a tough boss, thereby creating connection and sympathizing with their position, yet without giving away the farm.

Letting Go Of Perfection

A friend of mine bought her first rental unit. This was based on my recommendations that she could move out of her studio rental apartment, buy a triplex or fourplex, live in one unit, rent out the remaining units, and have virtually no housing payment. One of her strong suits is that she is very particular about how things are maintained. That is a great quality, and one she should maintain in the areas where she has direct control.

Yet one of her big growth areas, as a landlady, has been to internalize that she cannot exercise any real control over her tenants and their pets. She can charge them when they move out for things that were not maintained up to her standards, but she cannot expect them to not have dishes in the sink, or to always take the amazing care of her carpet, especially after that third glass of red wine that is just waiting to get knocked over. That is what security deposits are for: repairing, and cleaning or replacing carpets that tenants chose not to value. If they chose to value and take care of the property, they should get their security deposit back. If they didn't, appropriate costs should be deducted, less the *normal wear and tear* that state law in Colorado dictates we cannot deduct from a tenant security deposit.

There was an incident that gave this new landlady fits. Her tenants owned a Great Dane. It was already a pony-sized dog, even though it was still a puppy. As it was teething, it chewed the stair railing to splinters. Essentially, what to me was a relatively large piece of wooden stair handrail, was an amazing toothpick, at perfect chewing height, to the oversized puppy. My landlady friend called me one evening completely frustrated and still in a state of disbelief. I couldn't help but chuckle—from my more uninvolved view, this was amusing, and would even make a great cartoon. In the end, a new piece of stair railing cost about $30; with six screws, sanding the ends smooth, and applying a couple coats of spray varnish, the problem was addressed, with the tenants footing the bill for one of the more expensive doggy toothpicks.

My friend's emotional turbulence far exceeded the cost of addressing this issue and its true severity. It is really important to know that tenants, by definition, are just not likely to be as emotionally invested in your property as you are. I used to travel on business a lot, and used to have a rental car every week. I must confess that in my testosterone-fueled mid to late twenties, I sometimes did things with those rental cars I would never consider doing with my own car. Who intentionally tries to catch air in their own vehicle? Tenants are just like me. The key is to charge an amount of money in rent and security deposit that covers the typical expenses, and wear and tear, that are just life when having other humans as our clients.

As one speaker, Bill Bronchick, said, "The greatest revenge is cashing somebody's check."

Landlording as a Path to Enlightenment?

This book is not about recommending that you convert to Zen Buddhism, and start an active meditation practice where you focus on non-attachment to stop letting the mismatch between your desires and expectations and the actual reality of life cause you suffering. Yet at the same time, many religious traditions, and maybe even one you might be interested in, teach some of this. I do feel that mastering the art of not letting my expectations cause me suffering, when they diverge from reality as they often do, is a valuable skill that has carried me through my career is a landlord.

The more often I am able to take the view of being the dispassionate observer, even in my own life, like I did when I laughed at my friend's description of the giant stair rail toothpick, the better off I am. The other choice I have is take the perspective of the involved person who is easily put into mental states of being disappointed, enraged and, otherwise, negatively emotionally charged.

The second choice, one that easily becomes a habit to where I no longer perceive the element of choosing, is not contributing to my psychological and physical wellbeing. I must see the big picture in those instances. I make $2,000 a year on this rental, and the tenants are going to pay for the new toothpick/railing with no objections. Why waste emotional energy on this matter? Other than that I never contemplated that this could happen, nothing irreparably bad happened.

It is important to remember that one of my greatest agonies today, often makes an amazing story in 5 years. Can I emotionally fast forward to five years from now, where I am sitting in a bar, telling the story, with a couple of extra gory details thrown in to embellish the story, and make it seem even more dramatic, suspenseful, and entertaining? Other groups try to listen in and join me and my admiring group in laughing about my folly and the ridiculousness of the entire situation. Let's learn to laugh today. We're cashing the checks today; why not also have the laughter today?

F*** Off Money and Your Success at Work and in Life

Having cash reserves go far beyond just having a balance of funds in the bank, and a monthly account statement to feel good about. There was the 6-unit apartment building I purchased when I was 25 and, a year later, sold for a $100,000 profit. Yes, I paid off my student loans. But more importantly, I had a sizable amount of money in the bank for a long time.

I called that money *f*** off money*. Essentially, that money allowed me to be more honest at work, and bolder in expressing disagreement with bad ideas put forward by colleagues and superiors. It allowed me to be more of a renegade, which is my natural style to do things the way I knew they were right, rather than just trying to fit the default company mode of saluting the corporate flag, regardless of how inappropriate the orders I was told to march to, felt.

Having that cushion of money allowed me to feel more comfortable with the prospect of getting fired for being the best version of me. I knew that if I were fired, I would be able to take care of myself and my family, even if it took a while to find my next paycheck. In the end, having that *f*** off money* didn't get me fired.

It actually helped get me promoted. I acted as more of a leader, as more of an assertive, results-oriented employee, who was committed both to the company and to my personal values. I actually increased my earnings because of that initial cushion of cash reserve. Plowing those increased earnings into growing my real estate empire, now has me in the position where I'm self-employed. I no longer have to deal with the moral quandaries my prior salaried job as an IT consultant sometimes exposed me to.

My career in that industry confirmed for me that there is truth in the old adage about consultants in general, that there is money in solving a problem, but there is far more money in prolonging it. My company was never as guilty of that as some of our larger national and international competitors, but it left a sour taste in my mouth that I was part of that industry at all. At the time, I was strongly focused on being part of the solution rather than being part of the problem. The beauty of my real estate portfolio is that it allows me to live in a different ecosystem: the things I think about and deal with, and the people I interact with, no longer force me to sit there and smile when I really have no desire to interact with individuals who put money ahead of values in their lives.

No you don't get there overnight, but you can get there if you start now. Just like the Chinese proverb about the best time to plant a tree being 30 years ago, you must decide now to act, so that you can reap benefits in the future.

Real estate is like many things that have a trajectory similar to compound interest. The near-term result returns are not that dazzling, which partially explains that many people don't enter the realm of real estate investing, or don't stick with it when they do.

You need to be decisive, courageous, and have staying power. Rome was not built in a day, and your real estate empire won't be either. If you don't start now, you will never be a minor or major real estate emperor or empress.

Money in the Bank is Peace of Mind

Many banks will ask for proof of cash reserves so that you're in a position to pay several months of mortgage payments if anything untoward were to happen. Whether or not you have such reserves, your landlord policy will typically have a loss of use provision and, if it doesn't come with one, you should ask for it. If fire or flood, or any other event that made the home unrentable were to occur, that insurance would make payments to cover the lost rent, allowing you to continue making your loan payments without going out of pocket.

Nonetheless, cash reserves are a good idea. Like the *fuck off* money I referenced, having cash in the bank makes you a happier, more secure person who sleeps much better. Plus, having reserves like that allow you to take advantage of the next great deal on a rental property when one happens to come along suddenly.

Furthermore, you never want to be in the position where you cannot have repairs made because you cannot afford to pay for them. I know of a person who insisted on getting a number of rental properties in a divorce. Two of those units developed roof leaks that destroyed drywall, dripped water on the laminate floor, and create mold every time it rains. This individual does not understand the importance of proactive maintenance, and claims that she cannot afford to replace or repair the roofs, even though I introduced her to a roofer who gave her a very fair bid.

She has been able to find tenants, illegal immigrants, who are willing to put up with how the property is, but she is charging below market rents, and is not able to be selective in order to get quality tenants who take decent care of her units. At some point, the repairs that will need to be made to roof joists, drywall, mold mitigation, the flooring underneath, and so forth, can easily be double the cost of just having addressed the roof at the first sign of problems. That is unfortunate, and not the situation any landlord should be in. Furthermore, her low rents put her in a negative cycle. She cannot afford to make the unit nice, therefore she has to charge less, which robs her of the money to make or even maintain the unit in acceptable shape.

Conclusion: You Can Do This

Housing is one of the fundamental human needs. Moreover, as our global population continues to grow, housing will always remain a high-demand commodity that tends to increase in value. Even as services from telephone support to tax preparation to medicine are increasingly performed offshore in low labor cost countries, real estate to serve the American population will always remain in the US. The case for the market is clear. Real estate is an enduring value proposition.

This book has shown you techniques for avoiding the mistakes I made while learning how to be a successful real estate investor. I won't even claim to pretend that this is a way of earning money where you can remain at home in your underwear, or where you can go out wearing all white clothing and never get it dirty. Real estate requires courage, analysis, and clear boundaries on the rules you set for tenants and contractors. Most importantly, it requires either some real work on your part, or some serious delegation.

Nonetheless, you can do well while doing good. You can create freedom—freedom, that from the vantage point of me 5 years ago, wasn't fully comprehendible. I was the working stiff, in the office by 8:30 or 9 a.m., and leaving after 6 p.m., making somebody else's dreams come true, and bemoaning the fact that there was so little time to accelerate the accomplishment of my own dreams.

Yet I stuck with it, and worked the equivalent of two jobs to keep my priorities on the radar. I did 5 things every day that moved my personal objectives forward. And, in the end, I conquered.

Ultimately, I got laid off at my IT job after a conflict with the CFO over what at its heart was about courage. He didn't have it, and I told him so. I was uncompromising that we have to seize opportunity and go with a daring move because, as our firm had learned so often, if we didn't, someone else would. He disagreed and vetoed a contract for a project that was approved by the client, except for the signatures as a formality. I was laid off my next day at work.

I chose never to return to the political infighting and unhealthy machinations of a corporate day job. Without having been inspired to buy real estate early on, and without meeting Bob and learning to really do so at a profit, I would never have managed to be the much more fulfilled, much happier, free individual I am now.

I look back and can only move into that tingly feeling of deep gratitude. This path was never a clear, linear, or predictable path. It was a path of challenges, soul searching, and bouts of serious internal resistance to my doing the things that have been most valuable to my growth.
It has also been a path of miracles. I have met the right person with the right help, right advice, or right referral at the right time. Sometimes, when I was ready to give up, the Universe gave me the ideal opportunity that made me discard the unhappy resolutions I made at 3 a.m. the previous night.

I have been blown away by the beauty of people who do the right thing even when they could have chosen not to. I have been mystified by the serendipity around health and illness. I once called in sick, feeling awful on a Monday morning I was to have been on a plane to a difficult out of state client and, that afternoon, dragged myself out of bed to make an offer on a property that has since become a core component of my portfolio.

I couldn't have planned this path for myself. Instead, I just bow in gratitude to the blessings of a magnificent Universe. I am still working on throwing away my thimble to better accept the Universe's blessings with a spoon, cup, bowl, or even a bucket, yet I know that I am already blessed.

Most importantly, I am reaffirmed daily that the real limits are not in the world out there but in my head. Once I transcend my own limiting beliefs, thoughts, and attitudes, some miracle will come to me that proves once again that anything good can happen when I pursue the path of being open to it.

Fleming Schutrumpf

As Esther Hicks says in one of her splendid affirmations: "Everything is always working out for me," and in another: "There is much love here for you."

May you know that everything is always working out for you. May this book help!

About Fleming Schutrumpf

Fleming Schutrumpf is a respected businessman, mentor, educator, writer, and speaker, devoted to helping people achieve their peak potential, personally and financially, and to achieve freedom from sub-optimal life situations.

Fleming grew up in Germany, South Africa, and the United States, and has visited more than 40 countries.

Fleming purchased his first real estate property at the age of 22, built his own house at age 23, and purchased his first 7 units of rentals by the age of 25.

Fleming's undergraduate studies in Cultural Anthropology and Masters in Business Administration and Masters in International Business honed a keen interest in how peoples all around the world earn livelihoods, and how there are different cultures around surviving and thriving centered around shared spiritual philosophies, corporate cultures, and nations.

Fleming worked many years as a business and IT consultant, helping identify and correct sub-optimal business processes. Fleming has helped substantially improve business cycle times and financial results, achieving revenue increases and cost savings in the millions of dollars. Fleming has applied similar versions of these principles in his own life and those of people he has mentored.

Fleming is committed to the notion that spirituality and good business can coexist, and is dedicated to sharing that message.

For more information, visit www.RentalRealEstateBook.com,
or write to:

Fleming Schutrumpf
PO Box 2492
Denver CO 80201
USA